# be human, lead human

"In her engaging, easy-to-read style, Jennifer demonstrates why her leadership thinking is on the radar of every top thought leadership organization today. This book is timely and relevant as leaders seek effective tools to thrive in a post-COVID world. To unleash the power of your leadership potential, read *Be Human, Lead Human* today."

**—DR. MARSHALL GOLDSMITH**
Thinkers50 #1 Executive Coach and two-time #1
Leadership Thinker and *New York Times* bestselling author

"Jennifer shares principles and practices of human leadership as well as compelling stories from professionals in *Be Human, Lead Human*. She reminds us that people skills are not soft at all; rather, they are essential to effective leadership and driving performance outcomes! Masterfully written and thought-provoking for new and seasoned leaders alike, *Be Human, Lead Human* should be on every organization's executive and professional development resource list."

**—YOLANDA ROYALL-WILLIAMS**
Vice President of People & Engagement at Wireless Vision

"In *Be Human, Lead Human*, Jennifer shares honest, witty stories of human leadership from her own career as well as stories from clients and colleagues. Nash is a thoughtful writer, a connected knower, and a servant leader. The post-pandemic world has blown the door wide open for a new, better way to lead. This book should be on every leader's shelf so they can take a deep look inward to help navigate the path forward as they lead their organization into the future."

—**DR. AVINA GUPTA**
Senior Principal: Leadership Development at Chick-fil-A

"*Be Human, Lead Human* is packed with actionable advice and tools to help you lead more effectively. You'll learn how to map your journey as a leader, assess your skills, and develop a strategic roadmap to inspire your team and achieve powerful results."

—**DORIE CLARK**
*Wall Street Journal* bestselling author of
*The Long Game* and executive education faculty
at Duke University Fuqua School of Business

"Through storytelling and a superlative ability to amalgamate the seemingly chaotic constructs behind the science of leadership, Dr. Nash provides accessible and practical guidance to leaders at all levels with an empathetic underpinning. Her narrative is forthright in word choice yet erudite in its well-researched and referenced work. An enjoyable and useful read at any stage of your leadership journey."

—**J. MANUEL OCASIO**
Chief Human Resources Officer at Luminis Health

"Leadership has long been celebrated and revered as a hero's journey. Now more than ever, the world needs leaders to be human at work so everyone else can be fully human too. *Be Human, Lead Human* is a must-have resource to evolve your leadership to include being a hero while being human in the twenty-first century and beyond."

**—CB BOWMAN**
CEO Association of Corporate Executive
Coaches (ACEC), Courage Consultant, MCEC,
CMC, MBA, BCC, speaker, author, facilitator

"Decades ago, people in leadership positions claimed great prowess in creating strategy and managing investor returns. People woke up to that shortsightedness. Leaders lead people! People drive the business; create new products and services; and develop, retain, and delight customers. Engagement numbers even before COVID showed a major motivation crisis throughout the world. Through engaging stories of real leaders who make a difference, Jennifer reminds us that it all comes down to listening, empathy, caring, and inspiring the people in an organization to be amazing!"

**—RICHARD BOYATZIS, PHD**
Professor at Case Western Reserve University
and co-author of the international bestseller
*Primal Leadership* and the new *Helping People Change*

"In *Be Human, Lead Human*, Nash shares detailed practices of human leadership using compelling stories from her professional experience, captivating the readers with thought-provoking insights that encourage them to transform their leadership techniques. Nash's book is an excellent resource for every organization's executive development program."

—DR. LILIAN AJAYI ORE
Chief Learning Officer, Top 100 Learning and Talent Development Executive, and Founder of GC4Women.org

# be human, lead human

## how to connect people and performance

jennifer nash, PhD

**LIONCREST**
PUBLISHING

BE HUMAN, LEAD HUMAN

*How to Connect People and Performance*

ISBN    978-1-5445-3342-1    *Hardcover*
        978-1-5445-3343-8    *Paperback*
        978-1-5445-3344-5    *Ebook*

*To J,*

*You help me feel loved, heard, understood, valued,*
*appreciated, inspired, and seen in this dance.*

*Love, J*

# contents

# foreword

When Jennifer invited me to write the foreword for her book, I immediately read her draft manuscript from cover to cover. It's so fun to have the pleasure of reading a book so compelling that I couldn't put it down. *Be Human, Lead Human* is one of those books—I love it!

Putting people at the core of leadership seems fundamental. But in my experience of leading thousands of people as CEO of Ford Motor Company and of Boeing Commercial Airplanes and Boeing Information, Space, and Defense Systems, it's precisely the idea of putting humans first that leaders most often overlook.

In *Be Human, Lead Human*, Jennifer offers a compelling solution to maximize human potential: Human Leadership. She illustrates Human Leader examples through stories from her own career and other professionals' experiences and provides actionable tools to help people grow as leaders and human beings. These tools form an integrated approach to Human Leadership.

As you'll read in Chapter 2, Jennifer worked at Ford during my tenure and so experienced our "Working Together"© principles, practices, and management system firsthand. In the chapter, she relays the deep connection between Human Leadership and "Working Together"—"people first, love 'em up." As she explores our "Working Together" management system and the leader's role to hold themselves and their teams responsible and accountable for creating and nurturing the "Working Together" culture to create profitable and sustainable growth for all the stakeholders, Jennifer reveals to us how Human Leaders, "Working Together" leaders, create value by proactively leading themselves, others, and the business to drive performance. They connect people with their work *and* each other. They create a culture where people feel seen, heard, and important.

Jennifer's research shows that exceptional performance abounds when people feel they matter. By bringing people together, leading hearts and minds, and serving all for the greater good, trust increases, engagement skyrockets, and morale soars. *Be Human, Lead Human* provides a personalized roadmap to becoming a more effective leader—a Human Leader.

Throughout my career, it has been an honor to serve others through leadership. Developing current and future leaders is a core value of mine, one which Jennifer and I are both passionate about. I am delighted to fully support Jennifer in helping leaders become the best possible versions of themselves and Human Leaders.

Jennifer's book is evidence-based, well-written, and inspiring. She interviewed and surveyed over four hundred leaders and executives over several years to create the Human Leadership operating model. I appreciated her relevant examples, clear and concise writing style, and thoughtful insights throughout the book.

Jennifer is a top executive coach, management consultant, and start-up advisor. In *Be Human, Lead Human*, she demonstrates how and why she's one of today's top leadership thinkers. Jennifer is a kind and humble human being. I can't think of a better human to write the book on Human Leadership than Jennifer.

*Be Human, Lead Human* is a must-have leader development resource for MBA programs, leaders at all levels, and executives. I highly recommend you put this book at the top of your reading list. I am so pleased that Jennifer is sharing *Be Human, Lead Human* with the world and am confident it will improve lives and make the world a better place for all.

—**ALAN MULALLY**

*Former President and CEO, Ford Motor Company*
*Former President and CEO, Boeing Commercial Airplanes*
*Former President, Boeing Information, Space, and Defense Systems*

# gratitude

First and foremost, this book simply would not exist without the nearly four hundred leaders, executives, and professionals I interviewed or from whom I received survey responses. Their perspectives and lived experiences bring the book to life through story, beautifully illustrate the human element, and enhance learning for readers. To each of you, I offer my deepest respect, gratitude, and appreciation.

I am exceptionally grateful to Alan Mulally, whose Human Leadership, inspirational presence, and life zest not only ignited the spark for this book, but also role modeled how I could be a better human being and leader myself. Alan was beyond generous in writing an amazing foreword for this book, and I'm deeply appreciative of his wonderful contribution. Heartfelt gratitude goes to Sarah McArthur, who freely shared her time and talents as a writing coach to help me enhance the reader experience; it was wonderful to "Work Together!" I'm so honored to have both Alan and Sarah's friendship, encouragement, and support.

My leadership actions, behaviors, and beliefs have been sculpted throughout my entire life by many different human beings, and for this, I am profoundly thankful.

Firstly, my loving parents Susan and Bob Nash, who taught me the values of hard work, sacrifice, and service. My first dance teacher Lisa Pelio, who taught me at age three that success is getting on stage and dancing your heart out even when it's really scary (the emerald green tutu strung with bright twinkle lights helped!). My first piano teacher Kathy Krueger, who helped me learn at age fourteen that practicing Rachmaninoff's fiendishly difficult Polichinelle over and over again really does create personal mastery.

The teachers at Eisenhower High School, especially English teacher Rol Crane who encouraged my love of reading global authors and created space for me to lead myself through reflective writing. My German teacher at Delta College, Dr. Andrejs Straumanis, a Holocaust survivor, who inspired me to choose compassion over contempt. My French and German professors at Central Michigan University, especially Maria Huettig, Janet Lein, Gilles Labrie, and Gisela Moffit, who helped me realize my dream of living in Europe at age twenty-one, igniting my wanderlust and love of connecting with people through language.

All of my amazing Michigan MBA cohort colleagues (Go Blue! 💙 💙), from whom I had the honor of learning and with whom I had the privilege of collaborating. My professors at the Ross School of Business at the University of Michigan, particularly Gautam Ahuja, Wayne Baker, Kim Cameron, Paula

Caproni, Jeff DeGraff, Jeffrey Sanchez-Burks, and Gretchen Spreitzer, whose research and courses revealed theory, strategic frameworks, and verbiage to articulate the human element of business and plenished my people leadership tool kit.

Each of my Case Western Reserve University DM and PhD cohort members: Dijo Alexander, Justin Ames, Chuck Bishop, Brad Brezinski, Cory Campbell, Natasha Conley, Arron Fraser, Allan Glass, Jim Hemsath, Don Isham, Rodolfo Jimenez, Chris Lamb, Andrew MacArthur, Manny Ocasio, Tarina Pettiway, Tony Scardillo, Karl Shaikh, Lavonne Slaton, Don St. Clair, Avi Turetsky, and Doc Warr. They are my family and have made me a better leader and human being through our interactions. I am so grateful our paths crossed. My professors at the Weatherhead School of Management at Case Western Reserve University, including my dissertation advisor and chair Richard Boyatzis and doctoral committee members Ellen Van Oosten, Melvin Smith, and Dave Aron whose expertise, guidance, and support of my work shaped my formation as a leadership and executive coaching researcher.

My talented colleagues in Dorie Clark's Recognized Expert (REx) community, who make the world and workplaces better through their leadership. These amazing humans offer inspiration, friendship, and encouragement through the roller coaster of entrepreneurial life. They are my tribe, and I'm so grateful for each of them.

It takes a village of people working together to bring a book to life, and this book is no exception. My immense gratitude goes out to these people:

The talented editorial team at Scribe Media, particularly
Hal Clifford, Nikki Van Noy, and Nicole Jobe, who helped me
incisively polish my words. My creative and ever-patient book
coaches Chas Hoppe and Emily Gindlesparger, who helped
me create clarity from chaos as I brain dumped through four
outlines and three vomit drafts. My project manager Darnah
Mercieca, who kept track of all the people and moving parts to
publish on time. My designer Amy King, who gave this book life
and personality through her beautiful cover artwork. *Everyone* at
Scribe Media who touched my book in some way and worked
tirelessly behind the scenes to deliver this book to the world.

Corey Seeman, Director of Kresge Library Services at the
Stephen M. Ross School of Business at the University of Michigan,
who kindly provided research support throughout the book.

The entire Michigan Medicine NeuroSport team led by Dr.
Andrea Almeida, who helped me regain my health after an inju-
rious car accident. To NeuroOptometrist Dr. Erica Carder and
her entire team at Chelsea Eyeglass Company, who helped me
see the world again. Nicole Pettibone at Great Lakes Psychology
Group, Ed Oliver at Tri-Covery Massage and Flexibility, and
the fabulous Peloton trainers who supported my physical, emotional, and mental healing through psychotherapy, physical therapy, sports massage, and cycling, stretching, pilates, yoga, dance,
meditation, core, walking, and strength classes. Thank you all for
helping me recover so I could get back to training and competing
in ballroom dance.

My best friends Lesli Agcaoili, Tracy McCrea, Vauhini
Telikapalli, and Roxanne VanLandingham, who are like sisters

to me and the friends you call at 3:00 a.m. when the world comes crashing down. They are my unending cheerleaders and encouraged me to keep going when it would have been easier to just quit, grab some popcorn, and binge-watch Netflix. I love each of them to pieces. To my friends and family, especially my sister Amy and niece Ella, whose thoughtful care box and cards offered hope, love, and laughter during my long recovery.

My talented team and partners at Jennifer Nash Coaching & Consulting, including Amy Anger, Joe Bedocs, David Ben-Porat, John Caldwell, Skylar Griego, Samantha Higgins, Abhirup Kondekar, Danielle Liss, Maya Maddaus, Scott Nadeau, Katie O'Brien, and Erin Ollila who do what they do best so I can focus on what I do best. I am grateful to each one of you and look forward to many more years of working together.

To the love of my life, my husband Jozsef Bedocs, who read every single word of each of four drafts and three outlines, healed many headaches, and kept things running on all fronts for our family while I spent thousands of hours over these last few years interviewing, researching, and writing. You have been by my side throughout this journey, helped me become a better human being, loved me to life, and showed me what it means to love fully and completely. Thank you for your patience, love, and support, for hearing, understanding, appreciating, inspiring, and seeing me, and for helping me feel I matter.

To you, dear reader. Thank you for buying the book, giving me your precious time, and investing in yourself and your leadership.

introduction

# the paper plate

I've never been one for taking the road most traveled by.

When the three leaders who were four levels above me told me they couldn't give my handwritten message on a paper plate to the CEO, it didn't sit well. Realizing they had opened the interoffice envelope containing the plate (despite its being sealed and marked confidential) also didn't go over well with me. Forcing me to take it back, thereby rejecting my humble contribution and silencing my voice, was the straw that broke the camel's back.

I took matters into my own hands. Despite being in the midst of the Great Recession with the economy collapsing, I decided to risk my job, income, and home. I resealed the white, picnic-style paper plate adorned with bright red, blue, and yellow Superman stickers in a new interoffice envelope, jumped in my Cobra Mustang, and drove over to Alan Mulally's office at Ford

World Headquarters. I delivered the envelope with its message of gratitude to Amy, his trusted assistant, and asked her to please give it to him.

In case you're wondering about the low-budget plate, the Great Recession happened in 2009. The housing market crashed, and people lost their jobs. Ford had recently mortgaged all of its assets, including the iconic Ford blue oval logo, to secure a $23.5 billion loan. Zero discretionary funds were available. In spite of this, my department wanted to host an appreciation day in an attempt to boost morale. Several leaders pitched in and purchased thin, white, picnic-style paper plates, kids' stickers, and Crayola markers. They set up tables in the hallway, scattered these items on them, and encouraged employees to write and deliver messages of appreciation to each other.

I wrote my note to Alan because I wanted him to know I recognized his efforts in saving Ford from the brink of ruin. It was important to me that he felt appreciated for the hard work of changing organizational culture, which had kept its foot on Ford's brake of progress for far too long. As someone who rarely felt seen, understood, appreciated, or heard during my entire twenty-five-year corporate career, I was determined for others to realize a different experience.

I arrived at my desk one morning to see a blinking red light on my phone. Checking my messages, I found a voicemail message from Alan. Shocked, I pressed play.[1]

Alan said he had a tear in his eye and wanted to let me know how much the handwritten plate with its message meant to him. I was amazed he took the time to call me, a people leader far down the ladder whom he'd never even met. His action demonstrated that despite my location on the organizational chart, I mattered.

A few weeks after that, the mail clerk dropped off a bulky interoffice envelope at my desk. Intrigued, I opened it. Inside were Ford swag and a handwritten letter from Alan on Ford stationery—with a heart around my name!

The CEO of a Fortune 50 company had drawn a heart on his thank-you note, shown on the following page. The man had shocked me twice now.

It made my eyes leak. Although I had been working for fifteen years, it was the first time in my career that a leader demonstrated they saw me as human. Never before had I seen such a workplace display of humanness like the one that heart around my name signified to me.

The contrast between Alan and the skip-level leaders' behavior was stark. The skip-level leaders wanted to stay in control, keep me in line, and maintain the cultural status quo. Alan, on the other hand, embraced my humble gesture and literally responded with heart.

## have you felt unseen, unheard, or unimportant?

I'm sure you've had similar experiences like I did with those leaders several levels above me. Leaders who exhibit toxic behaviors such as silencing voices or disrespecting boundaries. Leaders who lead through power, fear, or command-and-control. Leaders who can't seem to open their ears, close their mouths, and truly listen.

Alan Mulally
President and Chief Executive Officer

World Headquarters
One American Road
Dearborn, MI 48126-2701 USA

Dear Jennifer,

Love my "Certificate of Appreciation"
Thank you!
And thank you for all you
are doing for our Ford!

Alan

5/2/09

→ Drive One
→ Fleet
→ Pens
→ Way cool Susan G. Komen
Scarf for you!

*Image description: A handwritten letter in blue ink on white Ford Motor Company official letterhead with the blue Ford oval centered at the top of the page. Letter reads: Dear Jennifer (with a heart encircling Jennifer), Love my "Certificate of Appreciation". Thank you! And thank you for all you are doing for our Ford! Alan 5/2/09. Note at bottom left reads: Drive One, Fleet, Pens, and way cool Susan G. Komen scarf for you!*

If you're honest, maybe *you* are that leader who silences others who disagree, or gets angry at colleagues for not doing what they're told, or feels they work harder than anyone else and wants others to step it up and care just as much.

Maybe you strive to be the hero. Yet somehow your heroic efforts are interpreted as toxic or insensitive. You feel pressure to always be right and have all the answers.

Despite your best efforts to connect with people, things just don't click. You make every effort to let people know you appreciate them, but it doesn't seem to land right. You want to be the leader everyone loves to work for, but people are leaving your team left and right. How can you become the people leader you want to be?

◄ ◄ ◄    **pro tip**    ▶ ▶ ▶

*If you are already an effective people leader, wonderful.*
*The world needs more leaders like you. I invite you*
*to continue reading and complete the Human Leader*
*Index (HLI). Perhaps you'll find a gem or two in there*
*that can help you take your game to the next level.*

▶ ▶ ▶   ▦   ◄ ◄ ◄

## becoming the leader others want to follow

This book is designed to help you upskill your leadership for the twenty-first century.

When you've finished reading, you'll understand how to be a more effective people leader. You'll evolve your leadership to become the leader people want to follow. You'll coach and facilitate others to maximize individual and organizational results.

Becoming a skilled Human Leader will help you improve productivity and communication and decrease stress. It will enhance your social and political capital and help you achieve desired outcomes. You will become the people leader you aspire to be and that the world desperately needs.

Throughout this book, you'll discover the principles and practices of Human Leadership. You'll acquire a new set of tools to advance your leadership. You'll learn how to lead yourself, rediscover and embrace your humanity, lead others humanely, and lead the business while infusing trust and safety into the workplace.

You won't be left hanging to figure out next steps on your own. You'll have the opportunity to assess yourself, learn where your skills currently land, and identify your goals. You'll walk away from this book with a strategic, clear, and actionable plan to bridge the gap. You'll take the first step to upskilling your people leadership capabilities.

## the long-lasting effect of a simple gesture

The emotional impact of Alan's handwritten letter today is as strong as the day I received it in 2009. It was the first time a leader showed authentic appreciation for me as a human being as well as for my work. Alan's simple gesture served as a catalyst for change throughout my life, leadership, and career.

It inspired me to reflect on my own behavior and how I helped others feel appreciated. It served as the impetus to write this leadership book and begin building my legacy. In addition, it deeply sparked my curiosity about why there aren't more leaders like Alan, driving me to earn an MBA at the University of Michigan followed by a PhD in Management at Case Western Reserve University.

**your turn**

Imagine the impact you could have on others with something as simple as a thank-you note.

As part of those studies and for several years after, I surveyed and interviewed over four hundred leaders and executives, including Alan, to better understand what gets in the way of effective leadership. I published and presented my research outcomes on leadership and executive coaching at Harvard/McLean Institute of Coaching and at Columbia University. I've shared my leadership thinking with Harvard Business Review, LinkedIn, and other media outlets.

This empirical, primary research informed my thinking for this book, shaped its framework and assessment, and inspired the stories contained within. I use this research daily in my consulting practice to help Fortune 50 executives build fluency in the human element of business.

Throughout twenty-five years in the corporate world, I worked for and with many leaders. I learned much about the leader I wanted to be and who I didn't want to be. Ever the student, I observed human behavior in organizations first as an employee, then as a behavioral researcher, and now as an entrepreneur, consultant, and executive advisor. I have been coaching Fortune 50 successful leaders and executives since 2010. What I know for sure is this: the world desperately needs better leaders.

## i'll spare you my dissertation, but share the wisdom

This isn't a fluffy, theoretical, or abstract ivory-tower book. It's not full of academic jargon. I didn't do a copy-paste of my dissertation (you're welcome). However, for those with unbridled curiosity, I have included curated learning resources in case you want to dive deeper into certain topics.

*Be Human, Lead Human* provides you with a personalized, strategic roadmap to elevate your people leadership skills. It assesses your current behaviors and provides operating tools to increase your capabilities. It offers tactical actions to improve your human and relational skills.

This book demands your presence and active engagement. It encourages you to leave the status quo behind. It dares you to break away from the pack and carve your own path. It challenges you to examine ineffective actions, behaviors, and beliefs keeping you stuck.

I've included several activities, called "Your Turn," which you'll see in the sidebars throughout the book. When you see them, I hope you stop reading long enough to focus on and complete the exercise. You'll also see my "Pro Tips" interspersed throughout, which are nuggets of wisdom gleaned throughout my corporate career as well as from coaching executives and consulting to organizations.

Every story in this book is true. However, some contributors opted to use real names and titles while others asked to remain anonymous due to company policy or for personal reasons. For those requesting anonymity, I have honored their ask and indicated such using an asterisk symbol after the pseudonym. Where stories were similar, I combined threads to create a colorful tapestry.

## why do i need human leadership?

Maybe you're wondering why now is the time for a shift or why what you've been doing won't work in the future. The bottom line is where you are as a leader right now is no longer effective. But it's okay if you don't know what else to do—that's what this book is for.

Massive operating environment shifts, unrelenting technological advances, and a global pandemic have forever changed the leadership game. Workplaces are constantly changing and will likely never be the same. What used to work will no longer get the same results. In fact, it will probably move you backward.

Human Leadership is an approach prioritizing people and is the new direction for leadership and the leadership solution for our new environment. I'll explain more about Human Leadership in Chapter 2. First, let's start by examining where we were in the past and where we no longer want to be. Turn the page, and let's get started.

1

# leadership today

## john's 360 wake-up call

**m**eet John*.

John is a forty-seven-year-old engineer working in the manufacturing industry. He is married, an empty nester, and has a golden retriever named Lucy. Like many white-collar office workers, he adapted to working remotely throughout the pandemic.

John has built a strong reputation by delivering projects and developing outstanding technical skills. He is comfortable focusing on tasks and prefers interacting with technology over humans. John was recently promoted to a people leader role. Although he's looking forward to a new role, he's facing several challenges.

Attrition in his department is high, his direct reports' engagement scores are low, business unit performance is subpar, and things aren't that great at home either. He's currently going through a divorce and has moved into a one-bedroom, spartan bachelor pad.

John considers himself a good leader, yet comments on his 360 report surprised him. He learned that his leader, colleagues, and direct reports think otherwise. While they appreciate John's bias to action (*what* he does), their comments reflect unfavorable observations of John's behaviors (*how* he does it) and beliefs (*why* he does it).

His 360 respondents mentioned John interrupts others and tells people what to do, gets angry when they don't do it, and talks over people. They also mentioned John's belief that it's his way or the highway. They shared stories of him yelling at direct reports in public, micromanaging their work and projects, and never admitting he's wrong. John is confused why this isn't working for him, since he learned these actions, behaviors, and beliefs from his previous leaders.

Like many leaders, John finds it challenging to make the shift from project to people leader. He struggles with changing his leadership actions, behaviors, and beliefs. His people leadership tool kit is empty, his 360 results are dismal, and he's at a loss on how to improve things going forward. Simply put, John is stuck.

## where are we now?

John isn't alone. Many people leaders face similar challenges. John's story illustrates three key factors limiting leadership today.

### Limiting Factor #1: Leading People (Actions)

*We are in a leadership pandemic.* As you'll see throughout the book, examples of ineffective leadership abound, from boardrooms to aircraft carriers to dental offices. Ineffective leadership didn't start with the pandemic but was certainly exacerbated by it.

The pandemic forced offices to close, which gave rise to remote work. These changes in how and where work got done meant leaders had to adapt their leadership actions. Many leaders lacked alternatives. But it wasn't just the pandemic that caused a dearth of options.

In his book *The Future of Work*, Jacob Morgan suggests there is a fifteen- to twenty-year gap between people leader promotion and training.[1] This gap partly explains why so many leaders struggle with the leap from managing projects to leading people. *Without coaching, proper training, or upskilling, leaders are left to their own devices trying to effectively lead people.*

Let's go back to John. As his story illustrates, John leads people as if they were inanimate machines and inhuman resources. But leading projects and tasks is vastly different from leading humans and hearts. John's actions aren't effective since people are human, not resources or project milestones to be achieved.

### Limiting Factor #2: Clinging to the Past (Behaviors)

By virtue of their role, leaders must embrace change for growth, which is the opposite of continuing the status quo. However, the majority of leaders steadfastly cling to the past. They continue to rely on tried-and-true behaviors even though circumstances, context, or roles have shifted.

As humans, we're wired to seek comfort and security over change and the unknown. Therefore, most people dislike change. The way "things have always been done" provides structure, promotes stability, and creates a sense of security. This is often why organizational status quo prevails—people fear change and the discomfort and uncertainty it brings with it.

For example, many leaders are more comfortable with in-person meetings rather than screen interactions. After months of seeing faces in one-by-one-inch boxes, CEO of JPMorgan Chase Jamie Dimon stated to CNBC, "I'm about to cancel all my Zoom meetings. I'm done with it."[2]

Jamie's comment reflects his frustration with virtual work practices and strong desire to go back to normal. But *clinging to how work has always been done reinforces the status quo.* Clinging to the past can have many unintended consequences—including lack of personal development, organizational stagnancy, and talent flight risk.

### Limiting Factor #3: Thinking Old-School (Beliefs)

John's story and 360 comments reveal his leadership beliefs and thinking. He believes in influence through positional power, managing through emotional volatility, and control through bullying. He thinks he must have all the answers, never fail, and always be the hero who saves the day.

Command-and-control leadership sufficed in the twentieth century for mechanistic tasks. However, it isn't as effective today for ambiguous and complex environments where human connection, communication, and empathy are paramount to effective outcomes. John needs to change his thinking to adapt to his current environment.

John isn't the only one who needs to shift his leadership beliefs. Remote work, also known as work-from-home (WFH), historically has gotten a bad rap. But despite Mercer's research suggesting that 94 percent of *employers* assessed company productivity the same or higher during the pandemic,[3] leader skepticism of WFH employees' productivity and engagement persists today.

CEO of WeWork Sandeep Mathrani commented in *The Wall Street Journal*, "People who are most comfortable working from home are the 'least engaged' with their job," and "people are happier coming to work in an office."[4] Goldman Sachs Group, Inc. CEO David Solomon stated in a CNBC article, "The (virtual work) arrangements are 'an aberration that the bank will correct as quickly as possible.'"[5]

Sandeep and David are not alone in their thinking. The Best Practice Institute's research shows 83 percent of CEOs want people back in the office as soon as possible.[6] Contrast that with just 10 percent of employees wanting to go back full-time and voilà—the perfect conditions for the "great resignation" storm of 2021.

This disconnect between CEO and employee thinking contributes to poor productivity and ineffective communication. Outdated thinking about where work is "best" done stifles employee voice, autonomy, and choice. Without a shift in thinking, *leaders who think work can only be done in an office may soon find themselves in an empty office without employees.*

## why are we stuck?

As the pandemic tsunami churned throughout the globe, decimating the status quo and obliterating life as we knew it, organizations tried valiantly to brave the waves of change. Leadership authorized remote work, changing the rules of engagement and redistributing the balance of power between employer and employee.

However, with the game change, leaders faced ambiguity and uncertainty. Lacking tools to navigate this murky new normal, leader actions, behaviors, and beliefs defaulted to leadership practices of the twentieth century, also known as status quo. Instead of reflecting, slowing down, focusing on people, and crafting a strategic way forward, leaders demonstrated a bias to action.

They rushed to reduce uncertainty with controlling styles such as micromanagement and authoritarianism. Their beliefs about what leaders "should do," how they "should behave," and what they "should think" drove ineffective leadership and removed the human element even further from the equation. Relying on control replaced responding with compassion.

John thinks he is a good leader. And he thinks he understands what leadership is. But *John is stuck because multiple environmental factors drastically changed while his leadership stayed the same.*

## what does this mean?

John is learning that a changing environment requires a change in leadership actions, behaviors, and beliefs. Without upskilling, growing, and evolving, John's leadership impact is limited. Ineffective leadership increases organizational turnover costs—to the tune of $630 billion in 2019 according to the Work Institute.[7] Recognizing the risk of insufficient people leadership competencies, the World Economic Forum identified people leadership as one of its top ten skills for 2025.[8]

David Hockney, owner of Ginger Group for Hair in Michigan, has been cutting hair for over fifty years. Trained under Vidal Sassoon in London, England, he learned early the importance of having the right skills and implements in his tool kit. David says, "You've got to have the right tools for the job. Straight-edge razor, blunt edge scissors, and geometric design are critical. Without them, I can't get the job done right or well."[9]

Like David without his hair-cutting tools, *leaders lacking Human Leadership tools can't lead people well.* When leaders lack the right tools for the job, culture withers, productivity plummets, engagement decreases, talent flees, and organizations fail. *To lead effectively, leaders must use the right tools at the right time.*

Sheldon Yellen, CEO of BELFOR Holdings, Inc., told *Insider*, "A company's most important asset is its people."[10] Sheldon's comment highlights how leadership must evolve for the twenty-first century. It's no longer about command-and-control, knowing it all, or posting profits. It's about leading people, focusing on hearts, and working together for the greater good. *Leaders must add a human element to their leadership tool kit to lead effectively going forward.*

# key takeaways

- Actions are "what" you do.
- Behaviors are "how" you do it.
- Beliefs are "why" you do it.
- Clinging to "how" work has always been done reinforces the status quo.
- Leaders who "think" work can only be done in an office may soon find themselves in an empty office without followers.
- Leaders don't have sufficient people leadership tools in their tool kits.
- People are human, not resources.
- We are in a leadership pandemic because the environment seismically shifted while leadership actions, behaviors, and beliefs stayed constant.
- Leading people requires different skills than leading projects.
- To lead effectively, leaders must use the right tools at the right time.
- Leaders need to add a human element to their leadership tool kit.

# 2

# the leader of the future

## going from red to yellow to green

**m**eet Alan Mulally.

Former president and CEO of Ford Motor Company and former CEO of Boeing Commercial Airplanes, Alan is a high-energy, humble, friendly, down-to-earth, and engaging human being. *Barron's* magazine proclaimed him one of the thirty "World's Best CEOs," *Chief Executive* magazine called him "Chief Executive of the Year," *Fortune* named him one of the "World's Greatest Leaders," and *TIME* magazine called him one of "The World's Most Influential People." A firm believer in lifelong learning, serving through leadership, participatory management, inclusivity, and continuous improvement, he answered Bill Ford's call to save Ford Motor Company.

When Alan arrived in Dearborn in September 2006, Ford was on track to lose $17 billion that fall. Bankruptcy loomed large on the horizon, and many things were not going well. Alan knew that his "Working Together" principles and practices could help turn Ford around, but he was up against a firmly entrenched hierarchical culture that lacked inclusion and the "Working Together" of all the stakeholders.

"Working Together" is an integrated system of operating processes, behavioral practices, and management principles designed to create value for all the stakeholders and the greater good. Its principles and practices shape how skilled and motivated teams work together, as shown in the following slide.

### our "Working Together" principles and practices

**our culture of love by design: skilled, healthy, and motivated teams**

- people first...love 'em up ♥
- everyone is included
- compelling vision, comprehensive strategy, and relentless implementation
- clear performance goals
- one plan
- facts and data
- expect the unexpected and expect to deal with it
- everyone knows the plan, the status, and areas that need special attention
- propose a plan, positive, "find a way" attitude
- respect, listen, help, and appreciate each other
- emotional resilience—trust the process
- have fun—enjoy the journey and each other

**creating value for all** ♥

*source: alan mulally © 2022*

Furthermore, "Working Together" clearly defines the leader's unique role, which is to hold *themselves and their teams responsible and accountable* for the "Working Together" operating process and expected behaviors.

Leaders fulfill this unique role by prioritizing people ("people first, love them up" ♥ ), developing and communicating the vision and plan with all the stakeholders, and transparently sharing the status of the plan's implementation. They create value by proactively leading themselves, others, and the business to drive "PGA," or profitable growth for all the stakeholders. Leaders create culture through connecting people with their work and each other. They drive engagement and commitment by helping people feel seen, heard, and valued.

The "Working Together" principles and practices shape healthy organizational culture and form one of the five elements of Alan's "Working Together" management system as seen in the following slide. The governance dimension refers to how the team manages itself, risk, and communication to remain aligned and on-plan. The leadership team includes all the company's leaders who are committed to the organization's vision, and to individual as well as collective responsibility and accountability. The creating value roadmap includes the vision, strategy, and plan. Last but not least, the business plan review (BPR) is a weekly meeting to review the business environment, the status and progress on the plan, and the risks and opportunities. Together these five elements create the "Working Together" management system.

Alan began implementing the "Working Together" management system and initiated weekly BPR meetings, where the leadership team reviewed about three hundred charts. Guests of each executive also attended these meetings, creating transparency and accountability and nurturing the "Working Together" culture.

**our "Working Together" management system**

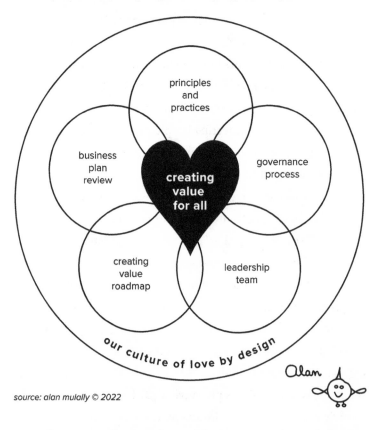

source: alan mulally © 2022

At first, every chart in the weekly BPR was color coded green for on-track. Alan told the team, "We're losing $17 billion. Is there *anything* in your area of responsibility that's not going well?" The all-green status went on for several weeks because people didn't yet trust the process of transparency and "Working Together." They didn't know Alan, and they didn't know what would happen to them if they shared an off-track status without a solution.

But soon, at a weekly BPR, Mark Fields, president of the Americas, presented his chart. It was color coded red for off-track. All of the air in the room disappeared. Everyone looked at Mark, then at Alan to see what he was going to do.

Alan stood up and started clapping. The executives thought, *There's the sign. The two doors behind Alan are going to open up, and two large human beings are going to come in. They are going to extract Mark, and so much for this "Working Together."*

Alan said, "Mark, that's great visibility. Thank you."

Alan then asked, "Does anybody have any thoughts about how to help Mark?" Derrick Kuzak was leading product development and said he had seen the SUV's failed liftgate latch before and would get Mark the data right away. Bennie Fowler was head of quality and said the same thing. Joe Hinrichs was leading worldwide manufacturing and sent engineers out to the Canadian plant to switch out parts and get production flowing again once they had a technical solution.

At the next week's BPR, all the charts were still green except Mark's. Alan couldn't tell the leaders what to do—that wasn't who he was as a person or the type of leader he chose to be. Alan knew they had to believe in and trust the process of "Working Together," and at some point, they would. A few weeks later, Mark's team had a solution, and his chart turned yellow. Soon after the vehicles started flowing around the world, Mark's launch chart turned green.

At the next BPR, the colors changed. All three hundred charts weren't green anymore, but a rainbow of reds and yellows and greens, and at that point, Alan knew the team had turned the corner. Everyone knew the reality of the situation, that it was now safe and expected to share issues and that they needed to work together to turn the reds to yellows to greens. In Alan's words: "This was a big deal and the big start of the fundamental culture change of 'Working Together' at the Ford Motor Company."[1]

Fast forward to when Alan retired in July 2014. Ford was creating and delivering value for all their stakeholders. Ford had become the number one brand in the United States and one of the fastest-growing brands around the world. Ford was recognized as the top brand to work for by all of the suppliers. Ford's employee satisfaction index had increased from 40 percent positive to 93 percent positive. Ford's stock price had risen nearly 1,400 percent

**your turn**

How do you think outcomes would have been different if John had been Ford's CEO during this crucial time?

from its low during the financial crisis.

Contrast Alan's powerful leadership at Ford with John's leadership in Chapter 1. Alan's leadership actions, behaviors, and beliefs are starkly different from John's. Alan manages his own emotional temperature, whereas John manages others through emotional volatility. Alan refrains from telling people what to do, while John micromanages and barks commands. Alan trusts the team to be experts in their space, but John considers himself all-knowing.

Alan facilitated Ford's stunning turnaround through his "Working Together" management system. First and foremost, he understood that to be successful in the complexity of the Ford environment, he needed to be a *coach and facilitator* to bring people together to collaborate rather than compete.

Alan also understood that many people are uncomfortable with change and the resultant ambiguity and uncertainty that accompanies it. To change Ford's culture, he knew he must lead himself first. He needed to be patient, maintain his emotional equanimity, and give people space to trust the process. Then he could coach others through the transition by helping people feel safe, facilitating relationships, and communicating behavioral expectations.

Leading through coaching, prioritizing and connecting people, driving engagement through honoring universal human needs, and creating value for all requires new actions, behaviors, and beliefs on the leader's part. Taken together, these changes form a new leadership philosophy and approach for the twenty-first century: Human Leadership. *Human Leadership is the leadership of the future.*

## human leadership

As I mentioned in the introduction, Human Leadership is a leadership approach prioritizing people. Grounded in a relational foundation, Human Leaders lead themselves, other people, and the business to create value for all. To deliver this desired outcome, Human Leaders integrate the human element, strategic focus, and relational connection as reflected in the following image.

## human leadership operating model

*Copyright Dr. Jennifer Nash*

Human Leaders act with a strategic, multidirectional focus. They focus on leading themselves, other people, and the business. They pay attention to the organization's internal heartbeat and the exogenous environment. Human Leaders stay up-to-date on current industry trends and understand how those will impact them, their team, department, business unit, function, and organization on multiple dimensions. They have situational, emotional, and social awareness and flex their style accordingly to meet contextual needs. They consider how their and others' decisions will impact not just them, but those around them. Simply put—Human Leaders are effective strategic leaders who focus holistically and systemically.

Human Leaders believe in prioritizing the human element. They see people as whole human beings with hearts, minds, hopes, and dreams rather than just employees. They understand people's motivations, strengths, and goals, and they align work tasks accordingly. Human Leaders lead themselves first, so they can lead other people and the business more effectively. They are inclusive and prioritize "all stakeholders," in keeping with the Business Roundtable's perspective on a corporation's purpose.[2] They believe organizations should be more than just places where employees come to work; they are also where people come to learn and grow as human beings. In sum, Human Leaders put people first and care about the whole human being and their needs, not just the employee.

Human Leaders behave in ways that build, nurture, and sustain relational connection. They create cultures that are healthy, preserve people's integrity, and promote risk-taking. They give trust first to get trust. Human Leaders build relationships through effective communication, authentic connection, and caring. They bring positive relational energy, compassion, and shared vision to interactions with others. In essence, Human Leaders understand that connection and relationships drive engagement and commitment, which in turn delivers performance.

Human Leadership is an integrated, holistic system of actions, behaviors, and beliefs designed to propel leadership into the twenty-first century. Human Leadership offers leaders strategic and humane practices to replace outdated styles, actions, and thinking in their toolboxes. It's time for leaders to leave the past behind, show up, and level up their people leadership.

## why is human leadership the solution?

Twentieth-century command-and-control leadership was designed for a simpler time when projects weren't so complex, environments so uncertain, technology so advanced, and direction so flexible. In today's world, this static leadership style is no longer effective. The dynamic nature of work requires leaders who can adapt, be fluid, and lead people effectively.

But leading humans is vastly different from leading machines or projects. When the COVID-19 pandemic of 2020 forced leaders to truly focus on people, it revealed the naked truth: *leaders simply don't have the necessary people skills in their toolboxes to lead people well.*

Combined with unrelenting technological advances, this effectiveness gap is a fatal flaw negatively impacting followers, leaders themselves, organizations, and the world. Research from MIT and Cognizant finds that *just 12 percent of respondents strongly agree* that their leaders have the right mindsets and beliefs to lead them forward.[3] Here are three reasons why Human Leadership is the optimal approach for today's leaders.

### Enabling Factor #1: It Helps *You* Grow as a Human Being and as a Leader

By its very nature, Human Leadership is a dynamic, engaged, and fluid approach to leading. As John's story shows, relying on twentieth-century leadership practices, or "the way it's always been done" no longer cuts the mustard. To become a Human Leader requires getting comfortable with uncertainty. It requires unlearning traditional actions, tried-and-true behaviors, and limiting beliefs currently in your leader tool kit.

The act of letting go requires change. However, while change creates loss, it also creates space. This space is ideal for reflecting on who you are today, who you want to be going forward, what being a leader means to you, how you want to lead people, and understanding your "why" for leading. Reflection creates the opportunity to know yourself, and knowing yourself is an *essential* characteristic of Human Leadership.

Just as reflection is not for those who dislike looking in the mirror, *Human Leadership is not for the faint of heart.* It demands courage to be true to yourself, conviction to behave in accordance with your beliefs, and clarity to pursue your purpose. In Alan Mulally's words, *"Who you are as a person has everything to do with who you are as a leader."*[4] Taking stock of who you are, who you want to be as a leader, and how you want to lead people helps you grow on multiple dimensions and transforms your leadership.

### Enabling Factor #2: It Helps *Employees* Grow and Evolve as Human Beings and Professionals

Human Leaders believe *people are the most important value creators in an organization.* Consequently, they put people first, are inclusive, and address universal human needs. As a result, organizational culture transforms into one filled with potential, possibility, and promise, where people enjoy working together, have fun, and accomplish meaningful work.[5]

When culture transforms, so, too, do employees' actions, behaviors, and beliefs. They know they matter and bring their wholehearted selves to work. They feel safe and are empowered to take risks through stretch assignments. They have autonomy, share their voice, and have a sense of ownership. They learn, grow, and evolve as a result of stretching, nurturing, and performing.

Human Leaders believe *organizations should be places where people come to grow, not just work.* This mindset shift has a positive effect on engagement, well-being, and relationships per Urrila's recent work.[6] It changes the nature of organizational culture to a twenty-first century model prioritizing people, relationships, and continuous improvement through learning. *Human Leaders help people grow and evolve on personal and professional dimensions.*

### Enabling Factor #3: It Helps *Organizations* Grow and Thrive

Research from Kim Cameron at the University of Michigan finds that when leaders put people first, organizational and individual performance increases.[7] Alan's story about the liftgate issue and prioritizing people supports Cameron's findings.

Research from Goleman, Boyatzis, and McKee supports Cameron's prior work. In *Primal Leadership*, they demonstrate that when leaders focus on people, organizational performance improves.[8] And the benefits don't stop there. Additional empirical studies have also suggested increased retention rates and decreased disengagement levels, along with improved morale and reduced negativity.

CEO of BELFOR Sheldon Yellen told *Insider*, "When leaders forget about the human element, they're holding back their companies and stifling a company's growth."[9] Like Mulally, Yellen understands that *when you put people first, performance and profits follow.* Putting people first drives performance because people feel valued. They feel *and* see that their leader cares about them, which increases commitment.

Olivia Croom,[10] a dentist and accomplished turnaround executive, says it well: "I'm all about the numbers, I really am, but you've got to care more about the people than the numbers, and they'll bend over backwards, they'll do anything for you." When people know you care, it changes how they show up and engage. Regardless of how challenging, dynamic, or unanticipated the exogenous circumstances are, people will go above and beyond to deliver when they feel valued.

## why is now the right time to be a human leader?

One year prior to the COVID-19 pandemic, 181 corporations agreed that the purpose of an organization had changed.[11] No longer was the primary purpose to make shareholders money. Rather it was more about prioritizing *all stakeholders*—including employees—and putting them first.

However, while they grasped the espoused theory, organizations struggled with how to act on this new paradigm. When COVID-19 appeared on the scene, it served as a forcing function to truly bring the human element of business to the forefront. Almost overnight, the COVID-19 pandemic revealed the 2020 leadership pandemic: unprecedented (people) leadership challenges without proper people leadership tools.

As we transition out of the pandemic and into a new leadership era squarely focused on leading people, leaders need to up their overall game. The complexity inherent in today's dynamic business environment will continue to grow at the same time the pace of change continues to accelerate.[12] To remain competitive, organizations need Human Leaders: leaders who prioritize people, recognize talent as a value creator, and bring humanity back to the workplace.

In his book *Talent Wins*, Ram Charan shares, "Talent has never been more important to an organization than it is today."[13] I fully agree. *You can't afford to not put people first.* From winning the talent war to delivering on performance objectives, success depends on you, your self-leadership, and your leadership of others.

*Looking ahead, the most effective and successful leaders will be Human Leaders.* Human Leaders are "vulnerable and courageous human beings; they lead other humans with compassion, kindness, and empathy; and they lead humanely by facilitating, showing love, and coaching."[14] If Alan Mulally, one of the World's Greatest CEOs, puts people first as a "Working Together" Human Leader (with actions, behaviors, and beliefs that saved Boeing *and* Ford Motor Company from the brink of ruin), shouldn't you be a Human Leader too?

## key takeaways

- Human Leaders coach and facilitate, rather than command-and-control.
- Leaders lack people leadership skills.
- Human Leadership is the leadership of the future.
- Human Leaders prioritize people.
- Human Leadership is not for the faint of heart.
- People are the most important value creators in organizations.
- Organizations are places where people come to grow, not just work.
- Who you are as a person shapes who you are as a leader.
- Human Leaders lead themselves, other people, and the business to create value for all.

3

# honoring the human you

### don't put your career GPS
### in airplane mode

**m**eet Markeshia*.
    Markeshia is a thoughtful, vibrant, and highly accomplished Black female director in a large global financial services organization. Over the last few years, she's built her brand as a turnaround leader and is now ready for promotion to senior director. A colleague of Markeshia's recently told her about an open role that might be a good fit.

By nature, Markeshia is risk-averse and conservative in her approach. She has carved out time over several weeks to conduct technical due diligence and ensure fit. She's been satisfied with the conversations she's had so far and is looking forward to learning more this week.

However, she recently got thrown a curveball. The CTO called Markeshia and personally asked her to apply for the role, mentioning it would only be open for another few days. The CTO told Markeshia he wants to fill the role quickly before next month's organizational restructuring. She suspects this is because he fears being transitioned out of the C-suite when the new leadership team comes on board.

Markeshia is torn because on one hand, she wants to get promoted, continue growing her brand as a turnaround leader, and gain visibility with the CTO. On the other hand, she is not excited about the role, tends to do what *others* think she *should* do, and is on the fence about applying.

When I asked her about it, Markeshia said, "This role is truly a stretch opportunity and a way to expand my skill set. It's not about the title for me—that isn't an effective carrot. I'm more interested in growing, learning, and being set up for success in this new role." She continued: "I think I could make it work, but I'm really not that excited about it. I just don't feel warm and fuzzy when I think about it." However, despite her internal GPS sending out warning signals, a few days later, Markeshia applied for the role.

What happened? Why did Markeshia apply for the role when she clearly wasn't passionate about it? Why did she ignore what she heard, felt, and thought about the role? How did she not hear the alarm bells going off, see the bright red flags waving wildly, or feel the hesitancy in the pit of her stomach?

Markeshia made a mistake I often see leaders make. She applied for the role because *she has been professionally trained to ignore the signals.* As a result, she dismissed critical data points her body sent her. These signals included her emotions, feelings, intuition, thoughts, instincts, and internal voice. It's as if she went into airplane mode and turned off her personal GPS.

When you turn off your personal GPS, it's next to impossible to tune into your human element. It's no wonder "tuning in" is challenging for most people. We're taught throughout our lives that technical or "hard" skills are "the best." They are the ones most highly prized and rewarded.

In contrast, human and relational skills are significantly less valued. They are the focus of MBA organizational behavior courses scoffed at by finance students. They are rated lower than technical accomplishments during performance reviews. And, as the epitome of disregard, they are referred to as "soft" skills.

However, there is nothing "soft" about human *and* relational skills; they are hardest to master and measure. Perhaps for these reasons, human skills development in the workplace is sorely neglected at our peril. *With so much focus on technical skill proficiency, we forget we need to be technically proficient about the human element too.*

One way to improve human element proficiency is to first honor our own human selves. In Markeshia's case, she was searching externally for data to help her make the role decision. However, she needed to turn on her personal GPS, trust her gut, and tune into her inner wisdom to make the decision, rather than relying on others to tell her what she "should" do.

And what happened to Markeshia in her new role? After the merger, a new CTO came on board and noticed Markeshia's lack of passion. Markeshia was moved out of the new role and ended up leaving the organization soon thereafter.

When you ignore the signals, you dismiss that which makes you human—your personality, reasoning, and abstract thought—and risk leading yourself astray. As Markeshia found, this can have undesirable consequences for your life, leadership, and career. But all is not lost—Human Leadership is still within your reach.

## how can i become a human leader?

As a leader, you are used to setting strategy, creating vision, and inspiring others to go on the journey with you. And likely you've done this throughout your career. But have you ever done this for yourself?

Many leadership books on the market today suggest that it's not about you as a leader; it's about your followers. I offer a different perspective. If there's one thing I've learned after my extensive experience leading people and coaching executives, it's that it must be about you first as a leader!

Why? If you can't lead yourself, no one will follow, listen to, or respect you. This won't help you gain a promotion, build credibility, or deliver results. You must *lead and manage yourself* before you can lead others. So what does it mean to lead yourself?

Four-time Olympic medalist Kerri Walsh Jennings is the most decorated beach volleyball Olympian of all time. Kerri says, "You have to lead yourself first and show up with all you have."[1] To lead herself and achieve success, Kerri clarified and held herself accountable to her values and goals, cultivated self-awareness, and leveraged a positive growth mindset.

Even though you may not be playing on sand and diving to make the dig, you can use Kerri's advice to land an ace in the office court as well. *To be a Human Leader, you must lead yourself first.* To show up with all you have, you must honor the human you. You must be in a relationship with yourself. You must find your way back to yourself and reconnect—something we all too often forget in the busyness of work and life.

Being in a relationship with yourself requires reflection— which can be uncomfortable, challenging, and difficult. The benefits of reflection have been studied for decades. Robert Greenleaf, who created servant leadership theory in 1970, suggests that leaders should "withdraw and reorient" themselves to effectively lead others.[2] More recent research from Giada Di Stefano and her colleagues proposes that leaders who reflect *perform 23 percent higher* than those who don't.[3]

Reflection involves digging deep to gain clarity on your life, leadership, and career. Are you ready to begin your Human Leader journey and lead yourself first? Let's get started.

## five steps to leading yourself first

The Human Leader journey follows a five-step path to honor the human you. To build the requisite human and relational skills to lead effectively, let's start at the beginning: by building you first.

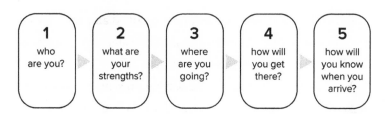

### Step 1: Who Are You?

To gain clarity on today's you, reflect on the path you've traveled to get to where you are today. Understand your values to clarify what's important to you. Discover your why to unlock the limitless energy that powers your life, leadership, and career.

#### *Your Life Dance*

Think back on the experiences and accomplishments that helped you get to where and who you are today.

- Consider *events* in your life, such as fighting cancer, your parents' divorce, or the death of a loved one.

- Explore the *circumstances* you experienced, such as being the only Asian in an all-white community, growing up in an alcoholic household, or surviving a global pandemic.

- Reflect on the *teachings* from people around you such as parents, religious figures, teachers, coaches, or leaders.

If you have a childhood memory box, scrapbooks, or journals, these items may offer reminders of your unique dance through life. How do these events, circumstances, and teachings impact your actions, behaviors, and beliefs today? Reflecting on what got you to today helps you connect the steps on your path through life.

**your turn**

Create your life dance map.

◄ ◄ ◄   **pro tip**   ► ► ►

*Google "life map" to see colorful examples or reference my Harvard Business Review article for a sample framework.[4]*

► ► ►  ▦  ◄ ◄ ◄

### *Your Values*

Values shape and guide our actions, behaviors, and beliefs. They help determine priorities and are how we measure life, leadership, and career satisfaction. When your actions and behaviors align with your values, everything feels right with the world. However, if there is lack of alignment, you likely feel unsettled, perhaps even anxious or dissatisfied.

Roland* is a bright, articulate, and successful executive in the banking industry. He loves cooking, cats, and Christopher, his husband of four years. Roland recently accepted a campus recruiting lead role for LGBTQIA+ students because he felt it was the right thing to do. However, he's traveling more for work recruiting trips and spending less time at home with Christopher. Roland isn't happy with this arrangement and feels like things are just "off"—at work *and* at home—since he took the new role.

Coming out during his college years and being an openly gay man at work, Roland knows firsthand the trials and tribulations of taking the path less traveled. Therefore, one of his values is supporting young professionals in being open at work. Yet with the new role requiring significant travel and more time away from home, Roland realizes his value of spending time with his family is a higher priority than recruiting.

He stepped down from the campus recruiting role. Shortly thereafter, he founded an employee resource group for LGBTQIA+ new hires joining his company. After finding a way to contribute at work and still spend quality time with his family,

**your turn**

Make a list of all of your values.

Roland felt like his values were again aligned in his life and career.

Values are what you stand for. Your behaviors are how you choose to demonstrate your values to others. For leaders, values are the foundation of their personal GPS. Without them, you can't pull out of the driveway of your life, leadership, or career.

### Your "Why"

Your personal "why" forms the foundation for your entire life. It serves as the limitless energy that powers everything you do. You derive meaning, purpose, and fulfillment from your why.

Often, our why is present from the very beginning of our lives. It's a common thread running through all of your life. It's the *reason* you do what you do. Think of your why as a motivator or driver underlying your actions, behaviors, and beliefs.

Some people love to take care of others—my sister Amy is a nurse practitioner who loves helping her patients grow and thrive. Other people love to cook—my mom, Susan, delights in sharing delicious, homemade desserts with her spry, ninety-year-old neighbors, Art and Phyllis. Others create art—such as domino artist Lily Hevesh—because they love the complexity, precision, and artistry of creating ten thousand plus–piece domino sculptures and sharing them with the world. Yet others—like Alan Mulally—lead because it's fun to serve others through leadership.

If you're having trouble identifying your why, think back to what you loved to do as a child. Maybe you played for hours with Legos, building structures or construct-ing cars. Perhaps you were fascinated with baseball or basketball, collected Topps cards of your favorite players, and memorized all of their statistics, like my brother Mike. You might have been a young Mozart, dedicating time every day to practicing scales and play-ing your favorite songs. Or you raised money like seven-year-old Bella Oakley of England

**your turn**

What patterns or similarities do you see between your childhood interests/ activities and chosen profession?

to make sure animals in Australia had food to eat during the wildfires, because her value was "to love and care for every coun-try all over the world."[5]

Identifying your why offers insight into why you do things the way you do them. Living in accordance with your why makes you a better human being. Leading with your why at the heart of what you do makes you a more effective lead-er—a Human Leader.

**your turn**

Articulate your why.

### Step 2: What are your Strengths?

What is a strength? *A strength is something you are good at and enjoy doing.* Researcher Marcus Buckingham suggests spending 75 to 80 percent of your time, energy, and effort using and building your innate strengths.[6]

**strengths diagram**

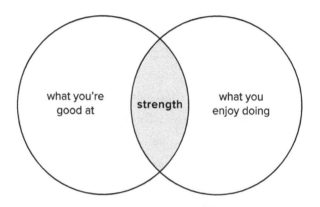

There are multiple ways to identify your strengths.

▪ Take a strengths test, like one of these: Gallup's CliftonStrengths;[7] the research-based CareerLeader;[8] the free VIA Character Strengths;[9] or the powerful Emotional and Social Competence Inventory (ESCI)[10] from Korn Ferry, created by Daniel Goleman and Richard Boyatzis.

▪ Ask people in your life what they think you do well.

▪ Reflect on tasks that put you in "flow."

Psychologist Mihaly Csikszentmihalyi describes flow as a state of being so contentedly engrossed in what you are doing that you lose track of time.[11] Being aware of what puts you in flow likely indicates a key strength. Spending time in flow is how you unlock creativity, innovation, and excellence in your life and work.

I'd be remiss if I didn't mention that strengths also can become weaknesses. *A weakness is an overused strength* in the wrong context. So it's just as important to identify strengths you're overusing and where they might be holding you back.

Here's an example. Charisse* recently moved from director to vice president of global audit in the consumer products industry. Auditing work requires exceptional focus to detail, and she's highly skilled at finding the needle in the haystack. But as vice president, her job is to set strategy and vision, not find needles.

Charisse received feedback that she's too "in the weeds" and that she hasn't shared any strategy with her team. The team is frustrated and feeling lost. With this new role and in this new context, Charisse's detail-orientation strength is not helping her move forward. It's actually holding her (and her team) back. She needs to stop flexing her detail muscle and build her strategic muscle instead.

Like Charisse has learned, *knowing your strengths is important because it helps you understand where you can be most effective.* Applying your strengths in the right context and amount contributes to fulfillment in your life and enjoyment in your work. Sharing your strengths with others contributes value to the world.

**your turn**

Make a strengths list and include those you overuse.

### Step 3: What Is Your Future?

The future you is the human being you envision yourself to be tomorrow, next year, or even ten years from now. In Step 3, you'll gain clarity on who you want to be and visualize your goals and dreams.

#### *Who Do You Want to Be?*

First, consider your responses in Step 1: Who are you today? Ask yourself if you are happy, satisfied, and content with today's you. Are you the best version of yourself today that you can possibly be? If yes, then skip to the Where Do You Want To Go section.

If you're not happy, not at your best, not sure, just want to explore a bit more, or don't know what you feel about today's you, that's okay! Take a few minutes to read the next few paragraphs and see if you can pinpoint what might be bugging you about today's you.

Often when leaders aren't content with who they are today, it's because they are going through an identity shift. Perhaps you've been promoted to a new people leader role like John was, but you know your skillset as a technical expert is better suited for project-focused work than people-focused work. And this new identity is a stretch—it feels really awkward.

Maybe you really liked who you were in your previous role—a superhero solving wicked problems—but in your new role, you're supposed to set strategy instead of save the day, and your ego is sorely missing the praise and recognition.

It may be that you are torn between who you are today, who others think you "should be," or what others think you "should do," like Markeshia with the pressure from her peers and CTO to apply for the role. It's common to struggle between who you are (your actual self), who you want to be (your ideal self), and who others think you "should" be (your ought self). Struggle stems from dissonance because your actions and behaviors aren't aligned with your internal values.

If you're truly honest, another possibility why you might not be happy with yourself today is your behavior. You know you're out of line when you publicly berate your dedicated employee sitting in front of you during lunch in a busy New York City restaurant, but you just can't seem to help yourself. Or you get angry and stomp around when coworkers don't do what you tell them to do, which is also exactly how you lose your temper with your kids when they don't behave.

**your turn**

Identify who you want to be and what needs to change to become your ideal self.

These examples hold people back from realizing their ideal selves. They are stuck in the past, instead of heading toward the future. These are examples of training, beliefs, behaviors, identities, external factors, or tasks that may need to shift to define the future you.

### *Where Do You Want to Go?*

I invite you to dream, and dream big. Focus your attention on your heart center. Take a few deep breaths in through your nose for four counts and exhale through your mouth for six. Feel yourself relax and get centered and your heartbeat slow. Close your eyes and continue this deep breathing for two minutes. Now open your eyes and continue breathing normally.

Ready?

Ask yourself *what you really, truly want.* This can be for your life overall, or you can get more specific by targeting your leadership or career. Regardless, I invite you to dream, tap into your heart's desire, and get clear about your vision and goals for the future.

Describe what you see in your mind's eye as you reflect on this big, audacious question about your future. Specify what you are doing as this future you. Describe your emotions as you see this playing out on your mind's movie screen. Engage all of your senses and include context such as perspective, location, and people as you visualize your future.

When you are ready, capture your future vision. Turn on your voice recording app and tell the story of your dream. Open Canva to create an electronic vision board or grab some magazines and a glue stick to go old-school. Compose and play an original song to tell your future story.

Research shows that elite, Olympic-level athletes use mental imagery to successfully achieve their goals and win gold.[12] Therefore, visualization is effective at driving performance. But if this seems too "woo-woo" to you, or you're having trouble visualizing, it's okay. Try the approach below instead.

- Reflect on your life dance map in Step 1: Who are You?

- Think of seven people throughout your life who positively or negatively influenced you. Describe who these people were and what role they played. List their actions, behaviors, and beliefs that you want to emulate or avoid.

- Compare and contrast their characteristics with your actual self—your actions, behaviors, and beliefs today.

- Consider how and to what extent you want to incorporate the positive attributes into your future vision of you and your life.

The pandemic served as a catalyst for many people to reconsider what is important to them, how they want to spend their time, and what they want from their lives, leadership, and career. Take this opportunity to reflect on your future vision. Connect with your heart's desire, dream big, and get clear about where you want to go.

**your turn**

Write down your future vision, your dreams and goals.

### Step 4: How Do You Want to Get There?

Determining who you are, understanding your strengths, and defining where you want to go provide the context, content, and direction for your future. Now it's time to determine how you want to realize your future vision. In Step 4, you'll prioritize your values and goals, identify resources, and create a timeline for your vision. Get a pencil and paper or e-device, and let's get started.

#### Prioritize Your Values

As you begin to lay out your plan, start with values. Remember, *your values are your internal GPS which guides your decision-making and behaviors.* When you live, love, and lead through values first, you achieve equilibrium and peace between your internal world and external environment.

Refer back to your personal values list in Step 1. Rank them

**your turn**

Prioritize your values.

in order of importance with one being highest and ten being lowest. For example, if you have ten values, number one might be autonomy, number two might be intellectual creativity, and number ten might be money.

### *Prioritize Your Goals*

Grab your goals list from Step 3 and review it. Draw three columns on a piece of paper and title them Life Bucket, Leadership Bucket, and Career Bucket. Write each goal on a separate sticky note and place it under one of the three bucket titles.

Take the Life bucket as an example. You have three goals in your Life bucket. Say you want to spend more time with your partner, climb Machu Picchu, and move to Bora Bora. Assign a priority to each goal, with one being highest and three being lowest.

To determine priority, ask yourself which value is involved, note its priority, and determine how important is the goal to you. Use low, medium, or high as measures.

If you get stuck, try using additional measures such as your

**your turn**

Prioritize your goals.

"why" from Step 1 (how it fits into your purpose), urgency (how soon you want to achieve the goal), expense (how much money you'll need to accomplish it), or preparation (how much time you'll need to train and prepare) to gauge priority.

### *Assess Your Resources*

Start with your Life bucket, goal number one. Identify the following three items necessary to realize your goal:

1. Resources you **need**
2. Resources you **have**
3. Your plan to fill any **gaps**

As you consider each of these three items, refer to the resource wheel below for thought starters.

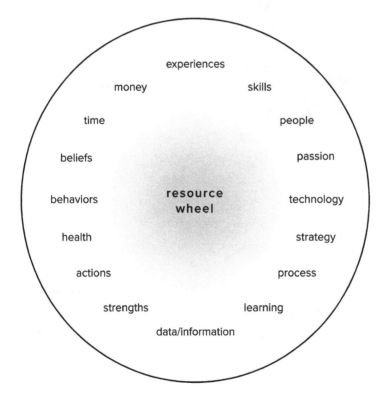

◄ ◄ ◄   **pro tip**   ► ► ►

*It's helpful to consider not only what you need to add, but also what you might need to let go of or subtract as you start on your future vision journey.*

► ► ►  ▓  ◄ ◄ ◄

Repeat the process for each life goal. Then move on to the goals in your Leadership bucket and finish with your Career bucket. You should now have a list of goals organized by priority and categorized by dimension.

**your turn**

Determine the resources you have and need. Create a plan to fill the gaps.

### Clarify Your Timing

Start with your Life bucket. Say your top priority goal is to climb Machu Picchu.

You've identified the following resources you have: available vacation days, money for the trip, and training time.

You know you need to lose weight, practice climbing, and have good weather when you are there.

To fill the gaps, you've decided to hire a trainer to help you lose weight, you're committing to go hiking every weekend, and you will schedule your trip during the dry season in Machu Picchu.

Now assign numbers to each identified resource and gap. Imagine you will meet with your trainer once a week for an hour each time over six months. Calculate that it will take you eight months to lose forty pounds at a rate of five pounds per month. Schedule twenty practice hikes over seven months. Plan on three hours to research and book the trip.

To build momentum, you decide to book the trip first since this will take the least amount of time. Now you have a travel date for your trip and can work backward from there. Add up all of the time for your Machu Picchu goal and enter it into Trello, Asana, or another timeline or Gantt chart–type solution. Repeat this process for each goal in each bucket.

**your turn**

Gauge time estimates for each goal.

### Step 5: How Will You Know You've Arrived?

Knowing you've arrived is just as important as knowing where you are going. Otherwise, how do you measure accomplishment? In Step 5, you'll define success, ensure sustainability, and think through accountability for your vision.

*Define Success*

Define measures of success for each goal on your plan. Perhaps it's simply completing the goal—full stop. Maybe it's a series of small behavior changes to create new habits.

Alternatively, it could be Fridays off if you're an entrepreneur, a stretch assignment, four hours a week to pursue a passion project, or 25 percent less stress in your life. Review each goal and determine what a successful outcome would look like for you.

◄ ◄ ◄ **pro tip** ► ► ►

*If you have leadership goals, don't wait until annual performance review time to evaluate progress. Gather performance feedback real-time from those around you. Savvy leaders go the extra mile and ask for one thing they*

*can do differently going forward. Understanding how others*
*perceive you informs your leadership journey progress.*

▶ ▶ ▶  ▦  ◄ ◄ ◄

### Sustaining Success

Sustaining success involves two elements: refraining from old behaviors and sustaining new ones. If your goal is to stop eating junk food, then don't buy Cheetos at the grocery store.

If your goal is to replace mindless snacking with mindful eating, then what new behavior will you replace it with? Maybe your goal is to drink healthy protein shakes instead. To sustain your behavior change, be sure to stock the necessary ingredients to make yourself healthy shakes.

**your turn**

Define success and sustainability measures for each goal. Form your accountability team.

### Accountability

How will you hold yourself responsible and accountable to achieving your goals and future vision? What will you do if you get off track with your plan? Define your accountability team members—the people in your life with whom you will celebrate accomplishments, share frustrations, and talk through failures.

## honoring the human you

Congratulations! You have taken the first step of leading yourself first and have begun the journey of honoring the human you. *The journey to Human Leadership starts with honoring the human you.*

These five steps offer a strategic, measurable, and timebound framework to help you grow as a human being. They create a heart-centered and purpose-driven plan for your life, leadership, and career. They allow you to be connected to and in relationship with your true self—a prerequisite for being in relationship with others, as we'll see in Chapter 4.

In addition, the Five Steps to Leading Yourself First offer an innovative approach to the entire talent life cycle. Developing yourself as a human being and a Human Leader is a lifelong journey full of growth and development, learning and change, joy and challenges.

To dynamically lead others in a changing world, lead yourself first with courage, clarity, and conviction. *When you're clear about who you are, where you want to go, and how you want to get there, you create the path to become the human and leader you are meant to be.*

## key takeaways

- We are professionally trained to ignore the signals.
- With so much focus on technical skill proficiency, we forget we need to be technically proficient about the human element too.
- To be a Human Leader, you must lead yourself first.
- A strength is something you are good at and enjoy doing.
- An overused strength is a weakness.
- Knowing your strengths helps you understand where you are most effective.
- Your values are your internal GPS guiding decisions and behaviors.
- Clear values, goals, and accountability help you become the human and leader you are meant to be.
- Human Leadership starts with honoring the human you.

4

# relationships: honoring others' humanity through human connection

## a PhD in collaboration and relationship building

**m**eet Geneva.

As the first female president and CEO of Detroit's United Way, Dr. Geneva Jones Williams is a catalyst for change. *Crain's Detroit Business* cites her as one of the city's most influential women. Founder and CEO of Dr. Geneva Speaks, she models her life and leadership values through her *Vibrant Life Blueprint*.

In early 2000, Dr. Geneva led the merger of two United Ways within metropolitan Detroit. With the successful merger under her belt, Geneva decided to complete her education doctorate at Wayne State University. However, local governmental leaders had something else in mind.

The mayor's office approached Dr. Geneva about leading multi-sector efforts to attract and secure national funding for Detroit. At the time, Michigan ranked forty-third out of fifty states in receiving available funding dollars, so there was ample opportunity for improvement. An experienced CEO, Dr. Geneva knew the risk of failure was high, but with millions of dollars at stake, so was the reward for success.

Dr. Geneva set aside her doctoral dreams and devoted herself to the City of Detroit and its people. She created a vision of public government, private foundations, and nonprofits working together. She knew the leadership skills this effort would require: bringing disparate stakeholders together, inspiring them to support the vision, and creating a safe space for collaboration.

She also knew that the only way to do this was through extraordinary relationships. Dr. Geneva explains her perspective: "If I could get people to collaborate and work together, this would build trusting relationships and increase investment dollars coming into the city to solve community problems."[1] This type of innovative, multi-sector partnership in an urban city was unheard of at the time.

Dr. Geneva rallied the parties around her vision. City Connect Detroit became an innovative national model of public-private cooperation. Within ten years, *they had secured more than $110* *million in federal and national funding* and established over forty initiatives to address community issues such as homelessness, food scarcity, fitness, health and nutrition, youth employment, and more.

How did Dr. Geneva achieve this impressive result? One word: relationships.

Dr. Geneva explains: "*Creating trusting relationships is not a passive activity.* Relationships are founded on trust, communication, and recognition. They require action, engagement, and commitment from all parties. Creating opportunities to work together such as planning work, assigning accountability, setting goals, and determining recognition creates strong relationships."

And what happened to her doctoral dreams?

Dr. Geneva feels it was divine intervention—she ended up focusing her doctoral work on collaboration and relationship building. The case study featured in her dissertation? City Connect Detroit.

Let's take a deeper look at defining relationships.

## how do you define relationships?

"*Relationships are the grease that gets things done.*"
—Priscilla, Leadership Development Consultant and former Fortune 10 Human Resources Executive[2]

"*Relationships define us: they are our backbone.*"
—Vauhini Telikapalli, Founder and CEO VEVA[3]

*"Relationships are foundational to success."*
—Graham, Founder and CEO of a boutique consulting firm[4]

These are just three definitions of relationships from leaders I interviewed. While each leader's definition was unique, they all shared a common element: growth. For Manny Ocasio, chief human resources officer at Luminis Health, the presence or absence of growth is key to determining the definition of a relationship.

Manny says, "Every interaction between two people has the potential to be a positive developmental event for both people. This assumes that you're in a relationship, that it's not just a transaction."[5] Being in a relationship means you're connected to, engaged with, and care about the other person. When you're in a relationship, you're on the same wavelength with someone; you relate to each other; you "get" each other.

Manny explains further: "When you have a series of transactions between people who are in a *transactional* relationship, one person gives and the other takes. But if you are in a *transformational* relationship, then each person shares and receives value, learns, and grows." Transformational relationships are developmental events for *both* parties.

This leads to the first key takeaway of this chapter: *Transformational relationships are the interaction and connection between two human beings, through which each person shares and receives value, learns, and grows.*

In contrast, *transactional* relationships are interactions between two human beings where one person "wins" while the other "loses." One person walks away with some type of benefit while the other receives nothing. We each have transformational *and* transactional relationships woven throughout our lives.

From conversations with the front desk staff at the doctor's office, to the grocery store clerk who (hopefully) puts your bread on top in the bag, to your mobile provider's support chat box, you interact with people each day. *Every interaction is an opportunity to reach out and connect on a human level.* We can tune in to connect and engage or tune out to disconnect and disengage. Relationships serve as the foundation of the HUMANS framework, which we'll explore more in Chapter 5.

## why are relationships important?

Tall and energetic with a warm smile, Bill Gryzenia is a successful CEO and entrepreneur with a track record of leading private equity-backed ventures to incredible growth. From Bill's perspective, relationships are how you drive opportunity.

Bill was incoming CEO at AxleTech in March 2015, a technology company focused on drivetrain systems and components for off-highway applications. His first day on the job, he received disturbing news: AxleTech had just lost one of its biggest customers—an account worth millions of dollars.

Bill says, "Everyone knew that the secret to success with this family-owned business was relationships. I knew the owners—the Taylor family—well because I'd visited many times before in my prior role as vice president of Aftermarket at Dana Corporation.

"The first thing I did was to start rebuilding the relationship with the customer. I made it a point to meet them in person, making many trips to their location over four and a half years. We would meet over coffee or for a meal."

Bill continues, "They wanted to sit down with me. They wanted to ask me questions and hear what I had to say. They wanted to get things off their chest and be heard. They wanted to meet my team and understand who they're dealing with."[6]

Bill shares the outcome of prioritizing this relationship: "Five years later when I left AxleTech, we were slowly winning back that business. We hadn't gotten back 100 percent of it, but we were up 80 percent, which is huge. *Relationships matter.* I understood that and made that a priority."

As you can see from Bill's story, *prioritizing knowing others and helping them get to know you is key to creating and sustaining positive transformational relationships.* He built trust with the customer by sharing his most precious resources: time, trust, respect, priority, and attention. This generated goodwill and desire to re-engage in a mutually beneficial relationship.

In essence, Bill used the Schein approach of "humble leadership" to rebuild the connection with his customer. In *Humble Leadership*, authors Edgar and Peter Schein define humble leadership as a personal approach to building trusted relationships.[7] Bill deftly leveraged this leadership tool as he worked to rebuild trust and connection with his customer.

As Bill demonstrates, one of the critical places we need human connection is at work. *Leading people requires connecting with people at a human level.* Connecting with people helps you drive results. Therefore, relationships are vitally important to individual and organizational outcomes.

Yet despite the importance of relationships, most leaders spend just 20 percent of their time on relationships per my research. For some, it's not on their to-do list because they view it as "extracurricular"; akin to a happy hour event outside of normal working hours. For others, particularly those in STEM fields, the importance of human connection is often overlooked in favor of hard numbers and quantifiable data.

However, human connection has benefits across multiple dimensions. Baym, Larson, and Martin point out that "relationships at work aren't just nice to have. They improve information flow, spur innovation, help retention, and (like Bill found) lead to better overall organizational performance."[8] *Positive, healthy relationships help people grow, organizations evolve, and humanity thrive.*

## what gets in the way of human connection and building relationships?

If leaders are spending just 20 percent of their time on human connection, then what are they doing with the rest of their time?

Leaders I interviewed spent 80 percent of their time on non-people-related work such as special projects, inefficient meetings, status reporting, and administrivia such as email and calendar management. With so much time spent on non-people-related matters, it's not surprising that leaders mentioned time as their biggest enemy to relationship building. Secondly, leaders cited a lack of interpersonal trust as a reason for not building connections. Last but not least, the leader's ego (self-focus) appeared as a factor in not building relationships. Let's examine these blocks to effective relationships.

## Time

Pat* is an engineer turned technical sales leader. Ever detail-oriented, he proudly pointed to his spreadsheet highlighting 82 percent of his time spent managing his team's work to meet departmental objectives. The remaining 18 percent of his day was dedicated to special assignments to elevate his capabilities and demonstrate his contributions to improving the business. With essentially 100 percent of his time spent on driving business results, Pat felt he was doing what he was paid to do—deliver results. He wasn't inclined to add an "unpaid" building relationships row on his spreadsheet.

**your turn**

*Actions*
Take a look at your actions. Review your calendar. What does it look like? Are you in back-to-back meetings all day? Do you ever say no to a meeting? To which activities do you allocate your twenty-four hours per day? What percentage of your time do you spend on building relationships?

*Behaviors*
Take a look at your behaviors. Are you often late to meetings? Do you forget about meetings? Do you cancel at the last minute or simply not show up?

*Beliefs*

Take a look at your beliefs and your ego. Dorie Clark shares in her recent TEDx Talk that "busyness is a form of status."[9] Do you flaunt your overbooked calendar like a badge of honor—taking pride in the fact you are double, triple, or even quadruple booked for every slot during the workday?

Now ask yourself: how is time getting in your way of building relationships?

## Trust

Vera* is a newer acquaintance of mine. Over the last year, we met several times in person for a meal. Each time we met, I sensed she had a wall up and that I was being judged. It was frustrating and uncomfortable because I neither understood her rampart behavior nor liked feeling scrutinized.

In between our lunches, there was little interaction. I liked Vera as a human being, but she didn't seem interested in getting to know me as a person. I was disappointed and disheartened by this, as I wanted to grow our relationship from acquaintances to friends.

After a year of these intermittent get-togethers, Vera suggested we meet for lunch at a local restaurant. When she arrived, she was clearly nervous. In a practiced speech, she told me all of the things she'd observed about me over the past year. Based on those data points, she asked me to play a significant role in her family's life.

All of a sudden, I realized why I felt so uncomfortable during our meetings. It's because I was being evaluated and judged! Without knowing it, I was "earning" her trust over the course of a year. And now she had deemed me worthy of a very big and very personal ask.

I walked away from that lunch meeting with exceptionally conflicting emotions. I was deeply honored that Vera would ask me to play such an important role. At the same time, I was deeply disappointed because she required me to *earn* her trust whereas I had simply *given* her trust.

Whether at work or at home, withholding trust inhibits relationships from day one. Breaking trust damages and often destroys relationships. Without trust, relationships cannot survive—they wither and die.

In contrast, giving trust is the cornerstone of strong and healthy relationships. It is the relational glue that creates generative interaction. It's the connective tissue that enables relationships to grow and thrive.

◁ ◁ ◁　**pro tip**　▷ ▷ ▷

*Proximity does not equal closeness or*
*connection in relationships.*

▷ ▷ ▷　▦　◁ ◁ ◁

As human newborns, we innately trust others. Yet, when we enter the workplace as adults, we are programmed to behave exactly the opposite. Through formal and informal cues, we learn that trust must be earned at work.

By withholding trust, we slow the relational process. We erect barriers to building connection. We dilute the relational glue.

In a world increasingly dependent on human connection, we

need to trust faster and more effectively to survive. *We need to get better at trusting others to foster human connection.*

### WIIFM ("What's In It For Me")

At twenty-five years old, Hugh Blane thought he had made it to the big leagues. The chairman of the board for a large organization recruited him to grow their portfolio of businesses. The chairman told him, "You're really smart, you're the guy, and I need you to get this done." Hugh went out and bought a new wardrobe and a new car. Hugh says, "I really thought that I was the big guy on campus. And since everybody respected the chairman of the board, I thought I could do no wrong."[10]

**your turn**

Think of the most recent person who had to earn your trust. What actions did they have to take to prove themselves to you? Did they earn your trust? How did that relationship grow (or wither) as a result?

Hugh hit the ground running. In fact, he ran over a lot of people in his zeal to perform and prove to the chairman he was "the guy." Within ninety days, the chairman pulled Hugh into his office and told him, "Let me tell you something, it's an amazing feat that you have done."

Hugh was starting to think, *Oh, I'm already going to get a raise.* The chairman then said, "It's amazing to me that within ninety days you have pissed off every single person in the corporate office. I got to let you know that I think that I've made a really bad decision. If you don't fix this in ninety days, I promise you, you're going to be gone."

Whether at work or at home, most people focus on what they can gain from relationships, rather than what they can give.

Hugh's story demonstrates a narrow WIIFM lens. *When you focus solely on gains to you, other people may feel used, unappreciated, or disrespected.*

Having a WIIFM focus makes it difficult for others to want to work with you. It makes trust difficult. Others may perceive you as selfish. And it makes it nearly impossible to build and sustain relationships.

**your turn**

Consider your relationships in all aspects of your life and work. Where do you use a WIIFM lens? How is this working for you?

## what tools and actions can you use to get better at human connection and building relationships?

Try the three tools and actions below to gain time, garner trust, and grow focus. With practice, they will improve your human connection and relationship building skills.

### Gain Time by Shifting Your Thinking, Actions, and Behaviors

Tarina, a leader in the financial services industry, says this: "Whether I'm meeting with my peers, a business partner, or one of my direct reports, those interactions all involve relationship building. *Everything* that I do is relationship building. To me, the work is the foundation for the relationship."[11]

To Tarina, *building relationships is not a separate activity outside of work: it is her work.* Leaders like Tarina are Human Leaders and chief relationship officers. Their entire responsibility consists of building, nurturing, and sustaining relationships. This focus helps people feel psychologically safe. It creates a trusting environment for people to thrive and perform at their best. It enables a culture of learning and risk-taking vital to growth, creativity, and innovation.

In short, relationship building is not a distinct activity from delivering work. It is an integral part of getting work done. Moreover, it is *how* work gets done. *Building relationships and getting work done are not mutually exclusive.*

To gain time, do these three things.

### 1. Shift Your Thinking about Your Leader Identity

Traditional or old-school leadership identity simply doesn't work in the twenty-first century. Leading with a "project manager," "chief problem-solver," or "the-buck-stops-here" identity no longer cuts the mustard. This is a post-pandemic, VUCA (volatile, uncertain, complex, and ambiguous), and digitally transformed world. We are dependent upon human connection and interaction for surviving and thriving. To lead effectively in this transformed world, put people first and be a Human Leader. View yourself as a chief relationship officer like Tarina.

**your turn**

Define how you want to show up as a Human Leader. Clarify your mission, vision, and purpose as a Human Leader.

### 2. Shift Your Actions Related to Your Leader Behavior

Clarify your role's responsibilities. You can't expect to have all the answers anymore. It's not realistic as complexity and the pace of technological change continue to increase.

As a Human Leader, you recognize, honor, and elevate the humanity in yourself and in others. You do this by inspiring others instead of controlling, coaching instead of commanding, and facilitating instead of micromanaging. *Human Leaders create space for people to grow together.*

For example, Trisha, a financial services leader, shifted her behavior during the pandemic. Since she wasn't in the office and no longer ran into people at the water cooler or in the cafeteria, she needed a different way to build relationships. She decided to set up a virtual huddle every Friday with her direct reports.

During the meeting, each participant shared high and low points

**your turn**

Identify the actions and behaviors you need to shift and change to become a Human Leader.

from their week. Trisha asked each person to identify needed support going forward. This regular interaction created opportunities to build relational connections. Qualitatively, Trisha and her team grew closer together and were more vulnerable with each other. Quantitatively, Trisha's team engagement score rose from 4.75 to 4.85, a 2.11 percent increase over 2020.

*3. Shift Your Perspective about People and Relationships at Work*

Which of these statements rings true for you?

- Your colleagues annoy you.
- Your peers are good friends you can't wait to see.
- Your boss is a narcissist who doesn't care about anyone but himself.
- Your leader has your back and never throws you under the bus.
- Your direct reports are simply "resources" to whom you delegate work.

- You enjoy getting to know your colleagues because they're interesting.
- You hate your workplace because no one accepts you.

As a Human Leader, your ability to deliver results (or lack thereof) is linked to engaging hearts and minds through transformational relationships. Human Leaders lead people through relationships. Human Leaders build high-quality relationships which shape organizational culture. In short, Human Leaders prioritize the human element to drive performance.

**your turn**

Identify your beliefs about people and relationships at work. Which perspectives need to shift to align with the Human Leader perspective?

◄ ◄ ◄   **pro tip**   ► ► ►

*If you'd rather interact with a screen or keyboard than do the hard and messy work of leading people, then you likely need a role or career change.*

► ► ►  ▨  ◄ ◄ ◄

### Garner Trust and Build Relationships into Your Work by Shifting Your Processes

Ellen is a financial professional in the insurance industry. During our conversation, she shared this: "I don't carve out time on my calendar just to build relationships. It's something I do during the course of my day."[12] Like Tarina, Ellen views herself as a chief relationship officer. She approaches each interaction with intention, focused on how she can start, build, nurture, sustain, or, if the situation warrants, stop the relationship.

Karl Shaikh is a strategic advisor, board member, and bestselling author. His most recent book is *Stop, Change, Grow: How to Drive Your Small Business to the Next Level.* He offers his viewpoint: "Literally every interaction is relationship development. The minute you enter a meeting, you're either starting, continuing, or closing a relationship. Say you enter a room of twenty-five people and three of those people you've never met before, so you're starting a relationship with those three. There are two people in that room you'll never talk to again—that's closing relationships. The other twenty people to whom you're presenting, hopefully you're improving your relationship bank account with them by being honest, providing value, sharing information, or asking better questions."[13]

Alan Mulally says this: "Working together and building relationships becomes how you operate—it's the status quo. You do it in the way you run the business: you start with a foundation of trust to develop and nurture relationships. *Relationships are absolutely key. Every interaction is an opportunity to develop the relationship.* When you have a process that everyone follows, an operating model, weekly business plan review meetings, and behaviors that go along with those principles and practices, you create and nurture trusting relationships."[14]

For Ellen, Karl, and Alan, time isn't an issue in building relationships because *it's built into how they operate.* Trust isn't an issue because it's built into their relational operating model. They foster relationships and get work done *at the same time* through their processes.

Make building relationships part of your day-to-day interactions and work processes. Show interest in each person by asking questions. Demonstrate that you respect them and their boundaries. Show that you care through your actions. Create a safe space for them to trust you and their colleagues.

**your turn**

Identify one change you will make today to integrate building relationships into your operating model.

### Grow Your Focus to Add Value to Others

Psychologist Adam Grant suggests that "success is increasingly dependent on how we interact with others."[15] When you are focused on you (WIIFM), at first you may succeed. But you will also be seen as a taker.

Being perceived as a taker has significant disadvantages. If you lead people, you may have high attrition, low engagement, and difficulty convincing people to join your team. No one wants to work for selfish leaders who take all the credit, realize all the benefits, and never give. Without a team, you won't deliver results and may be invited to join your organization's alumni ranks. If you don't want this to be your fate, shift your behavior and thinking.

Instead of solely realizing personal benefits, *consider what value you can offer to others*. Different ways to add value to relationships include being generous, exuding positive energy, giving encouragement, sharing information, asking thought-provoking questions, providing advice, insight, or guidance, highlighting industry trends, connecting others to key decision makers, listening or lending an ear, and many more. People will notice your behavior shift and likely respond positively.

Instead of taking credit, give credit where credit is due. Olivia Croom, whom you met earlier in Chapter 2, says, "A good leader doesn't have to get the credit. As long as you get great outcomes, people will understand it was your leadership that engendered these great results."[16]

Remember Hugh from earlier in the chapter? Let's take a look at how he grew his focus.

Hugh's boss, the chairman of the board, suggested he buy Dale Carnegie's book *How to Win Friends and Influence People*. Hugh dutifully bought the book, even though he thought "it was the biggest bunch of malarkey." But he rationalized the purchase by telling himself he was in Mayday mode. Hugh talked with his mother about the situation, who recommended he speak with Chris, a healthcare consultant in her network.

Hugh explained the whole situation to Chris. Chris then asked Hugh, "In this position, are you there to serve your own interests or the interests of all the employees, customers, and stakeholders?"

This question stopped Hugh in his tracks. For the first time, he considered that everything he had done was all about him and his ego. He admitted to Chris, "I think it's about me."

As a result of the conversation with Chris, Hugh shifted his thinking and behavior. He took Chris's advice and went to each person in his office. He let them know he knew he had ruffled feathers and pissed people off. Hugh asked each person for one suggestion about what he could do to improve his relationship with them.

Hugh thanked everyone for their feedback, stopped making statements, and started asking questions. He focused on giving to other people instead of growing his own ego. He learned it's always about the people he's serving: the employees, customers, and all back office support staff.

**your turn**

Choose one relationship in your life. Identify one action to contribute value to the relationship. Specify how and by when you will contribute this value.

What happened to Hugh? He wasn't fired; rather he learned how to *build connections by giving value to and serving others.* Three years later, Hugh was recruited for an even larger opportunity because of how successful he and his team were at the chairman's organization. In Hugh's words: "I would never have been successful if Chris had not come along and helped me learn how to put my ego in check."[17]

*Relationships are built on the human element, not transactional intent.* Focus on giving rather than receiving. Like Hugh, you'll likely end up with way more in return.

## concluding thoughts

As I write this, we are not just experiencing a global health pandemic. We are in a pandemic of a different nature—a human connection pandemic. Although technology brings people together more than ever before, it also creates division through screens. *We are quickly losing the ability to connect at a human-to-human level.*

When we don't connect with each other as human beings, we are in grave danger of losing our humanity. We risk losing empathy and gaining apathy. We risk decreasing social connection and increasing loneliness. We risk enjoying togetherness and augmenting division.

Losing the ability to connect is literally a matter of life or death. As social creatures, we can't live without relationships. *Just like children can't grow without love, adults can't thrive without relationships.*[18]

Employees perform at their best when they feel in relationship with their employers and bosses: connected to and valued by them. Engagement and performance operate in tandem with relationship quality and the cultural environment in which employees work. *Relationships honoring an individual's humanity are the currency that fosters connection, growth, and results.*

## key takeaways

- Transformational relationships are the interaction and connection between two human beings, through which each person shares and receives value, learns, and grows.
- Every interaction is an opportunity to connect on a human level.
- Leading people requires human-to-human connection.
- Relationships help people grow, organizations evolve, and humanity thrive.
- Trust first to foster human connection faster.
- The leader's role is to build, nurture, and sustain relationships.
- Building relationships and getting work done are not mutually exclusive.
- Every interaction is an opportunity to start, stop, or continue a relationship.
- Grow connection by giving value to others.
- Relationships are built on the human element, not transactional intent.
- We are losing the skill of human-to-human connection, thereby putting humanity at risk.

# 5

# HUMANS framework & human leader index overview

Which elements of your people leadership approach did you recognize in John or Alan, or in any of the leader stories shared in previous chapters? You may be asking, "How do I know if I'm a Human Leader or not?" Great question—keep reading.

## HUMANS Framework

I created the HUMANS (Hearing, Understanding, Mattering, Appreciating, iNspiring, Seeing) framework based on my empirical research with over four hundred leaders and executives. It consists of six elements designed to help leaders elevate their self- and other-leadership capabilities. This strategic, cross-disciplinary framework is based on principles of human behavior, psychology, neuroscience, communication, motivation, change, and relational connection.

The word relationship stems from fourteenth century French meaning connection.[1] Relationships connect humans with other humans. The elements of the HUMANS framework catalyze relationships, which grow when nurtured or wither when neglected. Therefore, the framework's six elements impact human-to-human connection, communication clarity, and interaction outcomes.

The six elements include **H**earing—hearing and helping others feel heard; **U**nderstanding—understanding and helping others feel understood; **M**attering—mattering and helping others feel they matter; **A**ppreciating—appreciating and helping others feel appreciated; i**N**spiring—being inspirational and inspiring others; and **S**eeing—seeing and helping others feel seen.

### HUMANS framework

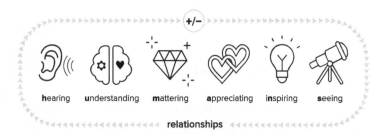

hearing    understanding    mattering    appreciating    inspiring    seeing

relationships

These six dimensions are universal human needs. They apply equally regardless of race, ethnicity, culture, geographic location, organizational level, gender, identity, ability, status, role, religion, or language. Furthermore, they are bi-directional. They use an internal and external or "self" and "other" focus, which my research suggests drives outstanding performance.[2] Human Leaders understand that meeting universal human needs positively impacts performance, while failure to do so has the opposite effect.

## human leader index (HLI)

Based on my rigorous research, the HLI contains sixty-seven questions addressing the six dimensions of the HUMANS framework and relational practices. It is designed to measure your leadership actions, behaviors, and beliefs. This will help you understand if your current leadership approach is more like John or Alan, provide a quantitative assessment, and offer guidance on how to advance your Human Leader journey.

**your turn**

Set aside a few minutes to take the index.

Grab a pencil or pen. Circle one answer for each question. (Don't worry about the point values now—you'll tally up your score at the end!)

To take the online HLI and receive a PDF report of your results, scan the QR code at the end of this book or visit *www. drjennifernash.com/behumanleadhuman.*

## HLI Questions

### *Instructions*

For each question, select the answer that is most like you, your actions, behaviors, beliefs, or leadership style.

### *Hearing*

1. I tell people what to do.

   ☐ Always  ☐ Often  ☐ Sometimes  ☐ Rarely  ☐ Never

2. I interrupt people before they finish speaking.

   ☐ Always  ☐ Often  ☐ Sometimes  ☐ Rarely  ☐ Never

3. When I am upset, I yell at people, disagree, or argue.

   ☐ Always  ☐ Often  ☐ Sometimes  ☐ Rarely  ☐ Never

4. I believe it's important to hear what people say.

   ☐ Strongly Disagree  ☐ Disagree  ☐ Neither Agree nor Disagree  ☐ Agree  ☐ Strongly Agree

5. I assume the worst about other peoples' intentions.

   ☐ Always  ☐ Often  ☐ Sometimes  ☐ Rarely  ☐ Never

6. I use my phone as a distraction while on conference calls or during family time.

   ☐ Always  ☐ Often  ☐ Sometimes  ☐ Rarely  ☐ Never

7.   I judge people negatively who think, behave, look, worship, love, live, lead, dress, speak, process, or act differently than me.

☐ Always      ☐ Often      ☐ Sometimes    ☐ Rarely      ☐ Never

**Hearing Total: _____**

## *Understanding*

8.   I understand what makes me tick.

☐ Strongly      ☐ Disagree      ☐ Neither       ☐ Agree       ☐ Strongly
   Disagree                          Agree nor                        Agree
                                      Disagree

9.   People accuse me of not hearing or listening to them.

☐ Always      ☐ Often      ☐ Sometimes    ☐ Rarely      ☐ Never

10.  It's more important for me to understand other peoples' viewpoints rather than tell them mine.

☐ Strongly      ☐ Disagree      ☐ Neither       ☐ Agree       ☐ Strongly
   Disagree                          Agree nor                        Agree
                                      Disagree

11.  I start responding in my head before the other person finishes speaking.

☐ Always      ☐ Often      ☐ Sometimes    ☐ Rarely      ☐ Never

12.  I understand what makes other people tick.

☐ Strongly      ☐ Disagree      ☐ Neither       ☐ Agree       ☐ Strongly
   Disagree                          Agree nor                        Agree
                                      Disagree

13. I am comfortable showing emotion at work.

    ☐ Strongly      ☐ Disagree      ☐ Neither        ☐ Agree      ☐ Strongly
      Disagree                          Agree nor                      Agree
                                        Disagree

14. I can control my emotional responses.

    ☐ Very          ☐ Untrue        ☐ Somewhat       ☐ True       ☐ Very
      Untrue           of Me            Untrue           of Me        True
      of Me                                                           of Me

15. I know my employees' strengths.

    ☐ Strongly      ☐ Disagree      ☐ Neither        ☐ Agree      ☐ Strongly
      Disagree                          Agree nor                      Agree
                                        Disagree

16. Understanding people helps me be a more effective leader.

    ☐ Strongly      ☐ Disagree      ☐ Neither        ☐ Agree      ☐ Strongly
      Disagree                          Agree nor                      Agree
                                        Disagree

**Understanding Total: _____**

*Mattering*

17. What matters is what others can do for me.

    ☐ Always        ☐ Often         ☐ Sometimes      ☐ Rarely     ☐ Never

18. It's important to help people feel they matter.

    ☐ Strongly      ☐ Disagree      ☐ Neither        ☐ Agree      ☐ Strongly
      Disagree                          Agree nor                      Agree
                                        Disagree

19. People tell me I make them feel insignificant or that they don't matter.

☐ Always  ☐ Often  ☐ Sometimes  ☐ Rarely  ☐ Never

20. I can name several ways I contribute value to other people.

☐ Strongly Disagree  ☐ Disagree  ☐ Neither Agree nor Disagree  ☐ Agree  ☐ Strongly Agree

21. I believe other peoples' lives are equally important as mine.

☐ Strongly Disagree  ☐ Disagree  ☐ Neither Agree nor Disagree  ☐ Agree  ☐ Strongly Agree

22. I enjoy helping others positively contribute to the world.

☐ Very Untrue of Me  ☐ Untrue of Me  ☐ Somewhat Untrue  ☐ True of Me  ☐ Very True of Me

23. I matter.

☐ Strongly Disagree  ☐ Disagree  ☐ Neither Agree nor Disagree  ☐ Agree  ☐ Strongly Agree

24. I have a fixed or closed mindset.

☐ Always  ☐ Often  ☐ Sometimes  ☐ Rarely  ☐ Never

**Mattering Total: _____**

*Appreciating*

25. I demonstrate appreciation to others at least once a day.

☐ Very Untrue of Me  ☐ Untrue of Me  ☐ Somewhat Untrue  ☐ True of Me  ☐ Very True of Me

26. Thanking people is common courtesy.

☐ Strongly      ☐ Disagree      ☐ Neither          ☐ Agree      ☐ Strongly
  Disagree                        Agree nor                      Agree
                                  Disagree

27. I specify what I appreciate about each person.

☐ Very Untrue   ☐ Untrue        ☐ Somewhat         ☐ True       ☐ Very True
  of Me           of Me            Untrue             of Me        of Me

28. Appreciating others takes very little time, effort, or energy.

☐ Strongly      ☐ Disagree      ☐ Neither          ☐ Agree      ☐ Strongly
  Disagree                        Agree nor                      Agree
                                  Disagree

29. I know how each of my employees prefers to be appreciated.

☐ Very Untrue   ☐ Untrue        ☐ Somewhat         ☐ True       ☐ Very True
  of Me           of Me            Untrue             of Me        of Me

30. It's difficult for me to show others appreciation.

☐ Always        ☐ Often         ☐ Sometimes        ☐ Rarely     ☐ Never

31. I have handwritten and mailed a thank-you note in the past
    year (not typed one via email).

☐ Very Untrue   ☐ Untrue        ☐ Somewhat         ☐ True       ☐ Very True
  of Me           of Me            Untrue             of Me        of Me

32. Employees need more than a paycheck to be appreciated.

☐ Strongly      ☐ Disagree      ☐ Neither          ☐ Agree      ☐ Strongly
  Disagree                        Agree nor                      Agree
                                  Disagree

33. I give credit to others where credit is due.

☐ Very Untrue    ☐ Untrue    ☐ Somewhat    ☐ True    ☐ Very True
  of Me       of Me      Untrue      of Me      of Me

34. People go the extra mile when they feel appreciated.

☐ Strongly    ☐ Disagree    ☐ Neither    ☐ Agree    ☐ Strongly
  Disagree             Agree nor          Agree
                      Disagree

**Appreciating Total:** _____

## iNspiring

35. Inspiring others moves them to act.

☐ Strongly    ☐ Disagree    ☐ Neither    ☐ Agree    ☐ Strongly
  Disagree             Agree nor          Agree
                      Disagree

36. I make people earn my trust.

☐ Always    ☐ Often    ☐ Sometimes    ☐ Rarely    ☐ Never

37. I know how to create a compelling vision.

☐ Strongly    ☐ Disagree    ☐ Neither    ☐ Agree    ☐ Strongly
  Disagree             Agree nor          Agree
                      Disagree

38. I have received feedback that I lack vision in current or previous role(s).

☐ Always    ☐ Often    ☐ Sometimes    ☐ Rarely    ☐ Never

39. Storytelling is a key leadership skill.

    ☐ Strongly    ☐ Disagree    ☐ Neither    ☐ Agree    ☐ Strongly
      Disagree                     Agree nor               Agree
                                   Disagree

40. It's easy for me to inspire others.

    ☐ Very Untrue  ☐ Untrue   ☐ Somewhat   ☐ True    ☐ Very True
      of Me          of Me      Untrue        of Me      of Me

41. It's my job as a leader to inspire others.

    ☐ Strongly    ☐ Disagree    ☐ Neither    ☐ Agree    ☐ Strongly
      Disagree                     Agree nor               Agree
                                   Disagree

42. People at work know the true/authentic me.

    ☐ Very Untrue  ☐ Untrue   ☐ Somewhat   ☐ True    ☐ Very True
      of Me          of Me      Untrue        of Me      of Me

43. To succeed at work, I conform to what others think I should look, act, dress, speak, think, or be like.

    ☐ Always    ☐ Often    ☐ Sometimes    ☐ Rarely    ☐ Never

44. People comment favorably on my storytelling capability.

    ☐ Very Untrue  ☐ Untrue   ☐ Somewhat   ☐ True    ☐ Very True
      of Me          of Me      Untrue        of Me      of Me

**Inspiring Total: _____**

## *Seeing*

45. In three (or more) of my last five conversations, I mirrored the other person's words or nonverbal body language

   ☐ Very Untrue   ☐ Untrue   ☐ Somewhat   ☐ True   ☐ Very True
     of Me      of Me      Untrue      of Me      of Me

46. I have had a colleague's office moved, or privileges and perks revoked as retribution for poor performance.

   ☐ Always   ☐ Often   ☐ Sometimes   ☐ Rarely   ☐ Never

47. I believe a person's value is more than just their output at work.

   ☐ Strongly   ☐ Disagree   ☐ Neither   ☐ Agree   ☐ Strongly
     Disagree                 Agree nor           Agree
                               Disagree

48. I purposefully or willfully ignore people.

   ☐ Always   ☐ Often   ☐ Sometimes   ☐ Rarely   ☐ Never

49. It's important to help others feel seen.

   ☐ Strongly   ☐ Disagree   ☐ Neither   ☐ Agree   ☐ Strongly
     Disagree                 Agree nor           Agree
                               Disagree

50. People comment that they feel invisible or unseen by me.

   ☐ Always   ☐ Often   ☐ Sometimes   ☐ Rarely   ☐ Never

51. I have at least three close friends who have different skin color, religion, or ethnicity than me.

   ☐ Very Untrue   ☐ Untrue   ☐ Somewhat   ☐ True   ☐ Very True
     of Me      of Me      Untrue      of Me      of Me

52. I ignore (or pretend to not see) people when walking past them.

☐ Always   ☐ Often   ☐ Sometimes   ☐ Rarely   ☐ Never

53. People seek me out to resolve conflict and bring people together.

☐ Very Untrue of Me   ☐ Untrue of Me   ☐ Somewhat Untrue   ☐ True of Me   ☐ Very True of Me

54. I place productivity and profits before people.

☐ Always   ☐ Often   ☐ Sometimes   ☐ Rarely   ☐ Never

55. I openly share my development plan with work colleagues.

☐ Very Untrue of Me   ☐ Untrue of Me   ☐ Somewhat Untrue   ☐ True of Me   ☐ Very True of Me

56. I can name the signs of stress, burnout, or overwork.

☐ Strongly Disagree   ☐ Disagree   ☐ Neither Agree nor Disagree   ☐ Agree   ☐ Strongly Agree

57. In the past six months, I have sent flowers, a handwritten card, or other gift to recognize a colleague's personal loss.

☐ Very Untrue of Me   ☐ Untrue of Me   ☐ Somewhat Untrue   ☐ True of Me   ☐ Very True of Me

58. In the last six months, at least one person has told me they feel seen or validated by me.

☐ Strongly Disagree   ☐ Disagree   ☐ Neither Agree nor Disagree   ☐ Agree   ☐ Strongly Agree

**Seeing Total: _____**

*Relationships*

59. People have to earn my trust; it's not freely given.

    ☐ Always   ☐ Often   ☐ Sometimes   ☐ Rarely   ☐ Never

60. I prioritize getting to know people.

    ☐ Strongly   ☐ Disagree   ☐ Neither   ☐ Agree   ☐ Strongly
      Disagree                   Agree nor              Agree
                                 Disagree

61. When it comes to relationships, I take more than I give.

    ☐ Always   ☐ Often   ☐ Sometimes   ☐ Rarely   ☐ Never

62. Relationships help everyone elevate performance.

    ☐ Strongly   ☐ Disagree   ☐ Neither   ☐ Agree   ☐ Strongly
      Disagree                   Agree nor              Agree
                                 Disagree

63. It's difficult for me to build relationships at work.

    ☐ Always   ☐ Often   ☐ Sometimes   ☐ Rarely   ☐ Never

64. I believe relationships at work are important.

    ☐ Strongly   ☐ Disagree   ☐ Neither   ☐ Agree   ☐ Strongly
      Disagree                   Agree nor              Agree
                                 Disagree

65. I spend at least 80 percent of my working hours building
    relationships.

    ☐ Very Untrue  ☐ Untrue  ☐ Somewhat  ☐ True  ☐ Very True
      of Me          of Me     Untrue       of Me    of Me

66. Building relationships and getting work done are not mutually exclusive.

☐ Strongly Disagree    ☐ Disagree    ☐ Neither Agree nor Disagree    ☐ Agree    ☐ Strongly Agree

67. I know how to build relationships.

☐ Strongly Disagree    ☐ Disagree    ☐ Neither Agree nor Disagree    ☐ Agree    ☐ Strongly Agree

**Relationships Total: _____**

**GRAND TOTAL (for all seven sections): _____**

### Your Results

Congratulations! You've finished the index. Now tally your score for each section and enter it on the "total" line beneath each section. Assign a point value to each of your answers using this rubric below:

- Always (1), Often (2), Sometimes (3), Rarely (4), Never (5)
- Strongly Disagree (1), Disagree (2), Neither Agree nor Disagree (3), Agree (4), Strongly Agree (5)
- Very Untrue of Me (1), Untrue of Me (2), Somewhat Untrue (3), True of Me (4), Very True of Me (5)

Next, add up your total score for all seven sections and enter it in the grand total line above. Locate your grand total score in the ranges below. Read your score description for your overall HLI results and next steps.

*Side note:* As a DanceSport competitor, I find that judges' scoring helps me assess my current proficiency level and pinpoint the technical, artistic, or cognitive skills I need to get to the next level. *Ballroom dance and leadership have much in common,* such as requiring flexibility and creativity, shaping and iterating vision, and initiating and responding to movement. These score descriptions are therefore dance-inspired. Whether in the ballroom or boardroom, I hope they inspire you and help you step up your performance.

- **Score Range 0–87: Warming Up.** Whether you're a young professional, new people leader, or haven't prioritized the human element in your professional development, it's okay! You're not alone. You may even feel like you have two left feet since you're not used to leading with human and relational skills first. Focus on what the possibilities are and visualize what can be different.

- **Score Range 88–164: Practicing Your Moves.** You've been trying out these Human Leader actions, behaviors, and beliefs to see what resonates. You're feeling more confident in your moves, but something still feels off. Create a strategic practice plan to help you find your groove.

- **Score Range 165–231: Making Smooth Strides.** You've mastered the basic steps in the Human Leader syllabus at this point. This has taken lots of practice, dedication, and hard work. Now it's time to work out the kinks. Keep breathing and stay on the beat!

- **Score Range 232–288: Dancing to Greatness**. You've shifted your Human Leader moves into muscle memory. You're delivering higher quality work, and your dance card is full of people wanting to salsa on your team. To up the tempo, add musicality and artistry to your leadership routine.

- **Score Range 289–335: Human Leader Virtuoso**. Your actions, beliefs, and behaviors reflect an outstanding Human Leader. You've mastered the flexibility and foundational technique necessary to shape and evolve your choreography as needed. Bravo!

### Results Interpretation

Consider your overall score as well as each dimension of the HUMANS framework score. Which dimension was the strongest for you? Where did you score the lowest? What surprises you about your scores?

Read the descriptions below to identify potential next steps. As you read, consider what actions, behaviors or beliefs you may need to shift and change to elevate your Human Leader performance.

#### *Your Level: Warming Up*
- Don't beat yourself up for dropping the ball, not being aware of these skills, or feeling like you're late to the

leading people dance. Acknowledge your humanity and show yourself some grace—it's okay.

- Don't try to fix everything all at once. It takes time to become fluent in the art of people leadership. Choose one framework dimension that feels doable. Pick one element (action, behavior, or belief) within that dimension, and give it a shot.

- Don't worry about being perfect and executing your moves flawlessly. Even JLo and Alan Mulally aren't perfect all the time. You do you, and learn what feels right for you.

### Your Level: Practicing Your Moves

- Pick one dimension. Map out a strategic plan to practice existing steps and add new moves to your dance repertoire. Be efficient with your time and targeted with your focus.

- If you're struggling to choose a dimension, look at your lowest score. Alternately, choose the one where you feel the most internal resistance. *(Pro tip: That's often what needs to grow the most!)* Or listen to what your gut is telling you to select.

- Focusing on one dimension at a time will improve your technique. As you gain proficiency, celebrate small wins and use that as encouragement to continue practicing.

### Your Level: Making Smooth Strides

- Although you're making smooth strides, it can feel like you've been practicing forever but still aren't quite ready for the ballroom. Take heart. The art of Human Leadership is a masterpiece that takes practice, skill, and patience.

- Reflect and take stock of how far you've come. Jot down your small wins and new steps in your life, leadership, and career. Acknowledge and honor your progress.
- If you're not satisfied with where you are, consider working with a coach to help you gain additional proficiency on your leadership dance floor.

### Your Level: Dancing to Greatness

- At this level, you might realize that you prefer to practice just the steps you do well. But to really cut a rug, you need to add more dimensional choreography.
- Share your HLI results with five colleagues, friends, or family members. Ask each to suggest three things you can do to get better at Human Leadership. Revise your strategic development plan to include these new moves in your repertoire.
- Kick up your heels and get to work on these challenging steps. Determine how and by when you want to master them to dance your way to people leadership proficiency.

### Your Level: Human Leader Virtuoso

- With all of the time, effort, and energy you've put in to get to this level, take a moment to celebrate your success. Congratulations!
- Recognize that not everyone has awareness of or facility with Human Leadership. Especially if you are a leader of

Human Leaders, you may need to support their upskilling efforts via coaching or mentoring.

▪ Consider how you can contribute to the world at large. Explore ways to share your dance of Human Leadership with others.

### Now What?

You've completed the HLI, received your scores, and reviewed potential next steps.

Now, here's where the rubber meets the road. Create a plan and write down the specific steps you commit to taking and by when. Share this plan with someone who will help you *hold yourself* accountable. Be sure to celebrate the small wins along the way as well as when you arrive at the ball!

Becoming a Human Leader can significantly elevate your life, leadership, and career. When you gain fluency in the human element, you improve productivity and communication, decrease stress, enhance social and political capital, and exceed desired outcomes. You become the people leader you aspire to be and know you can become.

To step into your best Human Leader self and learn how to excel at leading people, keep reading. The six dimensions and relational foundation of the HUMANS framework awaits.

◄ ◄ ◄ **pro tip** ► ► ►

*Refer back to your plan and add insights and learning as you see fit. Let's dance!*

► ► ► ▨ ◄ ◄ ◄

## key takeaways

- Leadership and ballroom dance share many common attributes.
- Relationships form the HUMANS framework foundation.
- Show yourself and others grace.
- You do you.
- Focus on one goal at a time.
- Make time to celebrate your accomplishments.
- To excel at leading people, practice Human Leadership.

6

# HUMANS framework: hearing

### just fifteen minutes greatly impacts the bottom line

**m**eet Ingrid.

Ingrid Tolentino, CEO of MetLife Legal Plans, is a highly successful, strategic, and visionary executive who has served in leadership roles for over twenty-five years. Ingrid began her career with MetLife in the strategy and services group of MetLife's Auto and Home business unit. Ingrid accepted the CEO role for MetLife's Legal Plans business unit in 2015.

5

Ingrid was very different from the previous CEO. He was an older, white male attorney, and she was a younger, brown female with strategic expertise. Their backgrounds, life experiences, and leadership styles had little in common.

One of Ingrid's first actions as CEO was to hold an "all associates" meeting. During this meeting, she shared her leadership philosophy and vision as well as her open door policy. Ingrid also announced that she wanted to meet with each associate for fifteen minutes.

She said, "Schedule time on my calendar, and come with your best friend if you're intimidated about coming by yourself, or come by yourself. I want to know three things: I want to know what's working well with the company now, what you think could be better, and what you want me as CEO to know."[1]

This open invitation to provide in-person feedback was dramatically different from the previous CEO's behavior. Associates weren't sure if they could trust Ingrid. Eventually the first few brave souls came into her office for their meetings and realized that, *Hey, it's a nice conversation. I'm not being terminated or let go; it's really just an open conversation.*

Ingrid ultimately met with ninety of the 110 associates, listened to them and captured their feedback through notes. It was a lot of time, but she knew it was important for people to share their perspectives and feel heard. Ingrid says, "That's what people really want. *People want the same thing: everybody just wants to feel heard.*"

Ingrid helped each associate feel heard by making time to meet with them, hearing their perspectives, taking notes, and making changes based on the feedback. This built trust and rapport early on. It also created record-breaking success for the organization.

Ingrid points out: "We grew at a rate we've never grown before and achieved amazing results. We nearly doubled revenue over four years. When I reflect on how we accomplished that, it's due to higher individual and team engagement levels, internal leadership-level promotions, strategic external new hires, and improved communication, relationships, and partnership with the broader MetLife organization. All of this happened simply because *I made time to hear each associate's perspectives* at the beginning of my tenure as CEO."

◄ ◄ ◄ **pro tip** ▶ ▶ ▶

*If you're a savvy Human Leader like Ingrid, you know that h-e-a-r are the first four letters of the word heart.*

▶ ▶ ▶ ▧ ◄ ◄ ◄

## what does it mean to hear others?

From a physiological standpoint, hearing means the act of perceiving with the ear or through an assistive listening device. When you hear others, it means you are aware of their speech sounds.

According to the Encyclopedia Britannica, the act of speaking creates an external sound vibration. Assuming healthy function, your ear transforms this vibration into an electrical signal or impulse. A neuron carries this impulse or electrical message to your brain. Your brain interprets this message as a sound, and voilà—you hear someone's voice and their words.

Figuratively speaking, hearing can mean: "I am hearing your words," "I am listening to you," or "I agree with you." (What? This isn't supposed to be a "woo-woo" book! Don't worry—we'll dive more into this later in the chapter!)

◄ ◄ ◄  **pro tip**  ► ► ►

*Hearing involves more than just your ears—it can also involve your other senses, mind, intuition, and body.*

► ► ►  ▧  ◄ ◄ ◄

Ingrid's story reflects what it means to hear someone from both physiological and figurative viewpoints. Ingrid intention-

**your turn**

How do you define hearing others?

ally carved out time to hear what her associates had to say about the organization's current and desired state. She created an open, accepting space for associates to share their thoughts. She not only heard their words, but she also asked questions, took notes and made operating level changes to demonstrate her commitment to their perspective. Hearing is the first skill in the HUMANS framework.

## why is it important to hear others?

From the research, interviews, surveys, and stories, the data is clear: Leaders who make the time to hear others and help them feel heard retain talent and drive outstanding results.

Brad Brezinski, founder and president of S2A, a consulting think tank, shares the story of a former boss who faced an unhealthy toxic culture when stepping into the CEO role. What did the boss do? Just like Ingrid, he introduced himself to people, asked questions and heard their perspectives.

What were the results? The leader realized a successful culture change. Attrition decreased, and morale increased. The organization hit their productivity goals ahead of schedule, within scope, and under budget.

Alan Mulally shared with me an example of how his "Working Together" process revolves around hearing others. Imagine you are in a meeting, and people are having side conversations. They aren't listening to or hearing the person presenting. What do you do?

Alan says, "You stop the meeting, and you look at them without saying anything. It doesn't take long before they stop the sidebar conversation. They notice everyone looking at them and quickly realize that they're not honoring the agreed-upon behaviors of hearing and respecting each other."[2]

Once the sidebar conversation stops, everyone's attention turns back to the presenter. The meeting picks back up. Consequently, everyone hears what the presenter has to say and the presenter feels heard.

What were the results of hearing others through Alan's "Working Together" process? By the time Alan retired on July 1, 2014, Ford celebrated a "fifth consecutive year of both profitability and positive automotive operating-related cash flow."[3] Ford never accepted a taxpayer bailout, its profits increased from a $12.7 billion loss in 2006 to profits of $6.3 billion in 2014, and its stock price increased 105 percent.

These stories show why it's so important to hear others. *Business results, leadership success, and healthy relationships depend on your ability to accurately hear other people.*

## what behaviors get in the way of hearing others?

Many behaviors hinder us from truly hearing the people around us. From earbuds crammed in ears while on the subway to talking over people in meetings, there are multiple ways we passively (or aggressively!) signal we really aren't interested in hearing others. My research with executives and leaders points to a triple threat of barriers: advocacy, assumption, and attention.

### Advocacy

If you have ever spoken out in favor of your preferred political candidate, recommended your spouse's favorite restaurant for dinner, defended women's rights, or protected someone from a bully, you've practiced advocacy. These specific examples reflect *selfless* advocacy: persuading *others* to support other people, places, concepts, or things for *others'* positive benefit.

In contrast, *selfish* advocacy is when you try to persuade others to adopt *your* beliefs, ways of thinking, or positions for *your own* self-validation, excuse rationalization, or ego's benefit. Which of these selfish advocacy scenarios sound familiar?

- Your aunt, who won't stop talking about her evangelical religious beliefs at holiday dinners or asking you when you're converting.

- Your dad, who's been watching too much fake news and is fixated on conspiracy theories.
- WeWork's CEO Sandeep Mathrani, who publicly announced his belief that "only the 'least engaged' employees want to continue working remotely."[4]
- Your neighbor, who believes that people of color are inherently lazy, would rather live on the dole, and just need to "pull themselves up by the bootstraps" and "get to work."
- Your micromanaging boss, who interrupts you when you're speaking and tells you exactly what you should do, think, or believe.

What makes *selfish* advocacy a barrier? It gets in the way because your attention is diverted—it's focused on *you* and *your* position rather than the other person. In other words, it focuses on benefits to you rather than the other person's gains.

With selfish advocacy, you say what you think is true, but that doesn't make it so. Even if you think your beliefs are best for you, it does *not* mean they are best for others. Leaders who demand others drink their Kool-Aid aren't Human Leaders—they're selfish advocates.[5]

**your turn**

Recall a time when you strongly advocated for a position. Now introspect. Was your motivation in the situation to benefit the other person, or were you trying to convince them to adopt your belief? Specify the type of advocacy you practiced.

### Assumption

Tarina, a leader in the financial services industry, got along well with her teammates. Her team was relatively young and still storming and norming to achieve high performance. They consistently refined their approaches and processes to adapt to their business customer's dynamic operating environment and priority shifts.

Over time, Tarina casually observed that some of her peers didn't appear to pull their weight when it came to tasks and quality project deliverables. Torn between her feelings about this and wanting to maintain good relationships with her peers, she kept her assumptions to herself.

When Tarina's manager accepted another position, Tarina accepted a promotion to manager, shifting the relationships from peer/peer to direct report/manager interaction. Once in the manager role, Tarina held one-on-ones with each of her nine team members.

Tarina asked her team members what they needed or were missing to deliver outstanding performance. When she heard their responses, she realized she had to suspend her assumptions. What she had interpreted as not pulling their weight was actually a lack of proper managerial support.

Tarina adds, "I had really questioned one of my team member's abilities to do her job. During our one-on-one, I heard what she needed from me as her manager, and I started providing the requested support. Within a short span of time, she blossomed and was actually doing a really great job."[6]

As a result, Tarina shared that what she's learned is that *"people want to be heard and know that you have their best interests at heart.* They want to feel like you're all on the same team, not just on 'Team Tarina.' You really have to provide the support that your team needs, otherwise they won't be successful, which ultimately won't make you successful."

Tarina's story about changing the way she perceived her team members highlights one of the barriers that gets in the way of hearing others. Tarina made assumptions about why team members were performing the way that they did. As so often happens, *when there is an information gap, we tend to fill in the story ourselves, just like Tarina did. Most often, that story is incorrect.*

**your turn**

Reflect on a recent assumption you made. What data did you have? What didn't you know? Identify the story you created to fill the gap.

### Attention

A while ago, I was leading an important presentation for a high-value client. All of a sudden during the meeting, my boss leaned back in his chair. He held his iPhone with two hands at eye level and *overtly scrolled through his email in the middle of my presentation.*

While he stopped short of kicking his feet up on the table, my boss's behaviors clearly signaled that he was not paying attention. This simultaneously signaled to the client that he didn't need to hear or pay attention to what I had to say either.

Due to his behavior, my boss didn't have to say a word. The client and I both observed and sensed that he wasn't attentive or present. I was shocked at the unprofessional behavior and frustrated at the lack of respect for me, and the client felt ignored. Needless to say, I left the company shortly thereafter.

Why is attention a barrier? Because when someone isn't attentive to you or mindfully present, like my boss in that meeting, you don't feel heard, and you tend to withdraw from the working relationship, organization, or interaction. *When we fail to pay attention, we pay dearly in missed opportunities to create connection, build understanding, and strengthen relationships.*

**your turn**

Think about the most recent interaction you had with someone. Were you fully attentive or distracted? How did you help (or not help) the other person feel heard?

To summarize these three barriers, you won't hear what others are saying if you advocate for your point of view, make assumptions, or fail to pay attention.

## how can you get better at hearing others?

We've covered three barriers that get in the way of your hearing others and helping them feel heard. Here are three solutions to remove these roadblocks.

### Inquiry

While writing this book, someone rear-ended me and totaled my car. It took quite a while for me to recover from my injuries and even longer to deal with the mountain of insurance and medical paperwork. As a result, I spent a lot of time in medical buildings, physical therapy, and doctors' offices.

Despite my general dislike of all things medical, I enjoy seeing my primary care physician, Dr. Greg Marcarian. When he comes into the room and asks me how I'm doing, it's not the perfunctory "How are you?" Dr. Greg is genuinely interested in what I have to say.

Dr. Greg gives me all the time necessary to share my story and is never in a hurry. I always leave the office feeling that I've been heard. This is also why I won't switch primary care physicians. Like dentists and car mechanics (oh, and husbands), when you find a great one, you stay with them.

Dr. Greg's habit of asking questions shows me that he is present and hearing me. Sometimes, his questions are closed-ended, to which I answer yes or no. Other times, he asks open-ended questions starting with who, what, where, when, why, or how. These questions lead to deeper information and data points, serving to inform his thinking and shape his diagnosis.

However, my best conversations with Dr. Greg (and others in my life) involve critical thinking via the Socratic method. Greek philosopher Socrates created this powerful methodology centuries ago. It forms the basis of my teaching and coaching philosophies, and it is commonly practiced in law and medicine today.

The Socratic method is a method of inquiry that invites clarity of thinking. It involves exploration of rationale, reasoning, and evidence. Perhaps most powerfully, it reveals blind spots, shines a spotlight on mental models, and surfaces limiting beliefs. After Socratic conversations, I gain either a new insight, a novel idea, an awareness of a formerly hidden assumption, or a new way of thinking.

What makes inquiry such a powerful tool? Inquiry shifts your attention to the other person and away from yourself. It demonstrates curiosity and a desire to hear and learn more about the other person's worldview, challenges, or successes. *Inquiry creates a sense of togetherness rather than divisiveness.* In these ways and more, it counteracts the advocacy barrier described previously.

### Fact-Check

Many leading news outlets such as CNN, *The New York Times*, and *Forbes* employ legions of people as fact-checkers. During the 2020 US presidential election, as candidates and the existing incumbent launched verbal arrows at each other, fact-checkers such as PolitiFact were busy behind the scenes separating fact from fiction.

PolitiFact is a not-for-profit national news organization. For the 2020 US presidential election, they fact-checked 1,443 election statements. Results showed that 39.6 percent of them had some degree of veracity ranging from "true" to "half-true." However, 60.4 percent had some degree of falsehood, from "half-false" to (liar, liar) "pants-on-fire."[7]

So what is fact-checking, and how do you do it? Fact-checking is a process of confirming an assertion's accuracy or truth. To check a statement's accuracy, there are many credible data sources you can use, such as think tank reports, academic research, industry publications, personal interviews, research databases, and more.

How does fact-checking counteract the assumptions barrier? When you collect data about a specific topic or situation, you use *evidence* to support or disprove the other person's position. This prevents you from making unfounded *assumptions* about the other person's statements, actions, behaviors, thinking, or beliefs.

### Paraphrase

How do you paraphrase? Let's use an example from a recent conversation with Carey*, one of my clients. Carey works in professional services and recently accepted a promotion. She was struggling to address a delicate and complex situation while maintaining her equanimity and peer relationships.

> *Carey*: "The topic I want to focus on today is how to appropriately have discussions with people about roles and responsibilities without offending them. I don't have any problem saying what needs to be said, but I don't want people to see how frustrated I am with them getting in my business and not staying in their lane."
>
> *Coach Jen*: "So let me make sure I understand. The topic you'd like to focus on today is how to have difficult conversations with people while maintaining your composure and positive working relationships. Is that correct?"
>
> *Carey*: "Yes—exactly!"

To paraphrase what Carey said, I had to (1) give her my full attention; (2) hear *and* listen to what Carey was (and was not) saying; (3) process her intended message; (4) state it back to her so she felt heard; and (5) invite her to confirm that my paraphrasing was correct.

Paraphrasing eliminates attention barriers because it requires laser focus on the speaker. It takes energy and attention to interpret and process spoken and unspoken messages. To effectively paraphrase, you must hear and listen to the speaker's words, vocal communications, and nonverbal communications.

## how can you help others feel heard?

The three tools of inquiry, fact-checking, and paraphrasing break down the respective barriers of advocacy, assumption, and attention. Now let's explore three actions to help you put these tools into practice.

### Be Curious

A client recently hired Allie and her team to come in and clean up the mess that several other consulting firms had left behind.[8] These other firms tried but failed to fully implement a new human resources system.

To learn why the other firms failed, Allie put on her curiosity hat and talked with different people throughout the organization. She discovered that (1) previous consulting firms didn't consider the *human element of change*, meaning end users' emotional, cognitive, or behavioral change impacts; (2) they didn't engage their *own* team members' hearts and minds in the project by helping them understand the big picture "why" of the work; and (3) they didn't include end users in defining, implementing, and iterating change processes, meaning the change was something that was done *to* them, rather than *with* them.

Armed with this information, Allie set out to do three things differently from her predecessors. She aligned each team member's work with their strengths, interests, and purpose. Second, she helped her team members get to know the end users as human beings by including focus group interviews as part of the project. Third, she shared the project vision and provided the big picture of how the work impacted the end users' lives.

By engaging project team members and hearing and involving end users, the team delivered a successful system implementation early, under budget, and within scope. Allie's story reflects that *there is power in ensuring that people feel their voices are heard*. When people feel heard and included, they are more willing to accept change. Engagement increases and new ways of working become the status quo.

Just as Allie and her team did through focus group interviews, I encourage you to be curious. Show someone you're interested in what they have to say by asking questions. Use open-ended questions starting with who, what, where, when, why, or how, rather than closed-ended questions that lead to a binary yes or no response.

**your turn**

Prepare five questions for an upcoming meeting. Challenge yourself to use inquiry rather than advocacy during the meeting. After the meeting, reflect on how your behavior change shifted your—and maybe even others'—meeting experience.

◄ ◄ ◄ **pro tip** ▶ ▶ ▶

*Most people love to talk about themselves. In fact, once you get them started, it may be hard to get them to stop!*

▶ ▶ ▶ ▦ ◄ ◄ ◄

Allie's story also reflects *how hearing someone humanizes them*. When project team members heard end users' stories, they engaged with them as human beings with faces, names, hopes, and dreams rather than as anonymous end users. They viewed them as whole human beings, as fathers, cat lovers, or movie buffs, not just employees.[9]

## Seek Out Facts

People feel heard when you ask questions. Asking questions helps you gather facts and data. Fact-seeking is powerful because it stops you from creating your *own* narrative about what someone says.

Furthermore, it prevents you from overusing a bias to action. Just as importantly, it hinders you from diving straight into problem solving without sufficient data. To get better at seeking out facts, try Dr. Barbara Gray's suggestion to separate out fact from fiction.

Chief librarian at the Craig Newmark Graduate School of Journalism at the City University of New York (CUNY), Dr. Barbara Gray is a recognized expert in fact-checking. She has over twenty years of experience researching news and is an associate professor of research methods at CUNY. Here are several of her tips on how to fact-check.

First, get clear about what a fact is. According to Merriam-Webster, a fact is something that exists, or a piece of objective information. For example, the statement "the moon orbits around the earth" is a fact. "Cows jump over the moon" is fictional. Separate fact from fiction, and identify what you need to fact-check through research.

Next, listen to someone's word choices. Listen for red flags such as "all," "only," "first," "best," or "worst." These superlatives lack specificity and inhibit reasoned argument. They may also suggest a lack of facts.

Finally, be aware of your own confirmation bias. Have you ever been in the market to buy a red car? Then, all of a sudden, you seem to see red cars everywhere you look? This is an example of confirmation bias—you're seeking information to confirm your purchase intent. For more on fact-checking, read Dr. Gray's suggestions for how to fact-check like a pro.[10]

**your turn**

Pick one topic you want to fact-check. Review Dr. Gray's suggestions. Conduct your fact-checking. What do you learn?

### Paraphrase What You Hear

David Craig, co-founder and CEO of GRYT Health, advises this: "If you're leading an organization into the future, the most important thing you can do is listen to the people that have been a part of it."[11]

**your turn**

In your next conversation, hear and listen to what the other person says (and doesn't say). Repeat out loud what you've heard so the person feels heard. Ask the person to confirm the paraphrase is accurate and if they feel heard. If the answer is no, what do you need to change?

As a seasoned leader, David understands that employees need to be heard. Even more importantly, they need to feel they are being heard. *As a Human Leader, David knows that the word "ear" is embedded in the word heart.*

Paraphrasing is a key communication skill and one every Human Leader should have in their tool kit. As the role of the future leader evolves into expert communicator, listening to people, recapping what you hear, and confirming accuracy is key to helping others feel heard.

## concluding thoughts

Hearing someone is one of the most important things you can do for success in your life, leadership, and career. When you hear people, they feel respected, valued, and validated. You gain awareness of *their* needs, worldviews, and experiences. You gather new insights and broaden your awareness and frame of reference.

Now that we've explored what it means to hear and help someone feel heard, let's take a look at deepening the comprehension of their words. We'll look at understanding in Chapter 7.

## key takeaways

- People just want to be heard.
- Hearing involves more than just your ears.
- Human Leaders attract and retain talent by helping people feel heard.
- Hearing others augments business results and engagement levels.
- Incorrect stories often fill information gaps.
- Inattention creates disconnection.
- Hearing someone humanizes them.
- Failing to account for the human element of change leads to failed transformation.
- Ensuring that people feel heard empowers them and you.

7

# HUMANS framework: understanding

## the importance of humanizing others

W e briefly heard from Allie in Chapter 6. Let's now take a closer look at what drives her success.

Allie Shobe runs a small permaculture farm, loves hiking and reading, and also happens to be an organizational transformation executive at Deloitte Consulting. Allie gets amazing results by treating people as humans first. She makes it a point to understand her team members' professional strengths and personal preferences. She artfully uses that knowledge to inspire top performance.

Earlier in her career, Allie quickly built her brand as a star performer. As an influential leader, people clamored to get on her project teams. It didn't take long for leadership to notice. Then the special project requests started pouring in.

Leadership asked Allie to turn around a failing project. Three different project teams over several years had tried without success to deliver a streamlined payroll system for a public sector client. Leadership asked Allie if she was willing to accept the challenge.

With "Adventurous" as her middle name, Allie decided to lean in and level up the project to victory. She quickly learned there were multiple red flags. The project team didn't understand the client's perspective, the client didn't have a voice in the project, and leadership wasn't transparent regarding expectations and deliverables.

Allie decided to craft a different experience. She started with transparency and an operating model built on trust. In Allie's words, "We invented our own way of working with folks. We made it a point to figure out what they do and don't care about."[1]

Allie viewed her biggest challenge as connecting the work's meaning, purpose, and impact with the interests of each stakeholder group. At the same time, gaining agreement to consolidate systems and find common contractual ground was paramount: *Allie needed to create shared understanding for all stakeholders.*

The challenge involved perception, communication, empathy, and knowledge gaps. Her project team members had removed the human element from the equation. They referenced end users as "resources" rather than as human beings impacted by the payroll change. Further, the project team didn't understand the day-to-day experiences of HR and finance employees using the payroll system. Leadership hadn't been upfront with communicating requirements, timing, and realistic deliverables.

Allie sent her team out to conduct focus groups with each stakeholder group. She wanted them to interact in person and hear firsthand what people cared about. And she wanted them to stop lumping the stakeholders into impersonal groups. Allie says it well: "*It's very easy to dehumanize people when you don't know who those people are.*"

Allie shares what happened next: "By stepping into the stakeholders' shoes, the project team gained empathy and made better decisions. Through personal connection, they created relationships, strengthened trust, and enhanced performance. It made them understand what we needed to communicate, how we needed to connect, and how to bring stakeholders on the journey with us. It humanized the whole project and made it about people rather than a system implementation."

Allie explains further: "We didn't want to do this payroll system change *to* stakeholders, we wanted *to join all of our energies* to figure out the best solution. We wanted to solve this together as a team, instead of making it an 'us-versus-them' activity. By the time we completed the project, the project team and the folks who were impacted were super aligned."

Allie smiled broadly and shared her highlight of the entire experience: "In all of my career, the biggest success is this project. We delivered this project successfully because we built the entire thing with and for people. I didn't do anything except *make it a priority to understand each person* and treat them like human beings."

In her words, Allie may have "only prioritized understanding each person," but this action created a fundamental dynamic that changed the game. Without understanding stakeholders and their unique perspectives, Allie's project would have failed like all the others. Dr. Ralph Nichols concurs: *The most basic of all human needs is to understand and to be understood.*[2] By meeting this elemental human need, Allie and her team delivered a successful project.

## how do you define understanding others?

Understanding someone is more than just knowing their title, location on the org chart, or employee ID number. Understanding someone means you gain insight into their reality and view the world from their perspective. Understanding others means learning who people are and what makes them tick.

In Allie's case, she needed to build understanding in multiple directions: Allie with team members; team members with end users; and Allie with end users.

To understand her team members, Allie asked them about their passions, purpose, and project preferences. She then aligned tasks with each team member's purpose. This demonstrated to team members not only that Allie heard them, but that she also listened and understood their perspective.

To help team members understand end users, Allie had her team conduct focus groups and individual meetings. By conducting live focus group interviews onsite, her team members met people in person and got to know them. They connected faces and stories with names. They reestablished the human element at the forefront of the project.

To understand end users, Allie gained perspective through focus groups and one-on-one interview data. Using empathy, she put herself in their shoes to recognize their feelings, learn about their culture, and gather insights about their viewpoints. She integrated this understanding and expectation setting into her communication of deliverables and timing.

These actions built three-way understanding. End users felt understood and valued by Allie and the project team. Team members actively engaged with end users as equal project team contributors. Allie set expectations and created shared understanding across stakeholder groups. This understanding and prioritizing human connection led to better stakeholder outcomes, higher individual and team performance, and increased bottom line results.

When you seek to understand someone else, you try to understand their feelings, thoughts, and perspectives. You want to know what is important to them, what they prioritize, and what their values are. You hear and listen to what they have to say, and you comprehend the meaning and essence of their words.

Understanding is the second skill in the HUMANS framework.

**your turn**

How do you define understanding others?

## why is it important to understand others?

Shira Miller is chief communications officer for a global supply chain organization.

Throughout the last few months, Shira and her team have been under intense pressure. They produced the company's annual report within a tight timeline. At the same time, they pulled together a new company video that has taken long hours over many weeks. The team's interactions and composition have also shifted due to remote work guidelines and the Great Resignation.

As if this weren't enough, Shira's department was tasked with communications for multiple enterprise-wide change initiatives taking place at the same time. Despite the team's best efforts, several communications didn't go out as planned, and things came to a head in a recent executive team meeting.

One of Shira's colleagues mentioned a missed comms deadline. Frustrated and stressed, Shira got defensive, lost her cool, and snapped at him. Shira explains: "I wasn't listening to his words; I was putting my own interpretation on his comments."[3]

Shira went home that evening and thought about what happened. She had interpreted her colleague's comment as a criticism, although it wasn't meant that way. Shira realized she was in her head and not truly listening to her colleague.

As a global communications executive, Shira gets paid to communicate effectively. Demonstrating a lack of technical expertise by misunderstanding this colleague's comment in front of the C-suite could have impacted her reputation. To make matters worse, she misunderstood the colleague *and* demonstrated a lack of emotional self-control—both of which hinder communication. Fortunately, Shira had built effective C-suite relationships so that her boss and colleagues knew Shira as a human being, not just as a hot-headed executive, and recognized this event as an outlier.

From this experience, Shira learned *it's important to pause and understand what others are really saying.* When we don't understand others, we miss opportunities to build connections. We interpret fact-finding as criticism. We make assumptions instead of asking questions. We seek flaws and find fault. We create division through words.

On the other hand, when we understand others, *we refrain from making assumptions, adding meaning, or creating division.* Often we *think* we understand what someone is saying. But in reality, we understand *our own interpretation* of what they've said.

◄ ◄ ◄  **pro tip**  ► ► ►

*When negative emotions are involved like in
Shira's example, all rational thought stops.
Fight, flight, or freeze instincts take over, and
understanding goes out the window.*

► ► ►  ▨  ◄ ◄ ◄

Shira used this personal example as a learning experience for her communications team. She shared with them what had happened during the executive meeting. As a result, her team members shifted their behavior. Instead of blaming others or covering up mistakes, they were honest about dropped balls and missed deadlines. They felt safe to ask for support. *Understanding others leads to effective communication, authentic relationships, and higher performance.*

# what behaviors get in the way of understanding others?

Shira's example demonstrates one behavior that inhibits understanding: failing to listen. Two other behaviors that block understanding per my research include being an empathy miser and emotional hijacking. Let's review failing to listen first.

### Failing to Listen

*"You're not listening to me!"* How often have you heard this phrase from your partner or someone else in your life? If you've ever said this to someone else, chances are neither of you were feeling understood.

*"Most people do not listen with the intent to understand; they listen with the intent to reply,"* says Stephen Covey.[4] Stephen's comment is an example of Shira's interaction with her colleague. Instead of listening and seeking to understand first, Shira responded with emotion in the heat of the moment.

**your turn**

Who most recently told you, "You're not listening to me"? Did you or they feel understood at that conversation's end?

Why does failing to listen stop you from understanding others? *When you listen with the intent to reply, you're no longer listening to someone else.* You're listening to yourself. Your attention is focused on the response you're composing in your head. This leads to misunderstanding, confusion, hurt, disappointment, and anger. It leaves both parties not feeling understood. And it can damage careers, relationships, and lives.

## Empathy Miser

Vishal Garg is CEO of Better, an online mortgage originator. In a stunning display of poor judgment, Garg fired nine hundred people via a one-way, three-minute Zoom call three weeks before Christmas. News of the firing spread quickly and went viral on social media.

Given the firing backlash, Garg issued an apology letter stating he "blundered" the firing execution. But the letter smacked of insincerity and was too little, too late. The board asked Garg to "take some time off."

Garg didn't demonstrate to laid-off employees that he truly understood or even cared about how the firing would impact them. Rather, he accused *them* of stealing from him and the company, according to *The New York Times*.[5] For the layoff survivors, Garg equally showed zero empathy, telling them that poor performance wouldn't be tolerated, per a *Vice* article.[6]

As a leader, Garg isn't known for his compassion, his tact, or understanding people. Per employees' comments in *The New York Times*, he uses foul language on conference calls.[7] *Forbes* stated he called employees "dumb dolphins" in an email.[8] Garg is an empathy miser.

How does being an empathy miser inhibit understanding? It erects connection barriers. In Garg's case, his lack of empathy had significant repercussions for Better. It damaged the brand (touted as the Best Startup of 2020[9]), created end-to-end talent life cycle

**your turn**

When could you have demonstrated empathy or compassion but chose the opposite instead? What factors prompted you to behave in this way?

challenges, and delayed and may have even canceled a $7.7 billion reverse merger, as reported by Axios.[10]

### Emotional Hijacks

Hank Schrader, the DEA (Drug Enforcement Agency) agent in Netflix's *Breaking Bad* series, is stoked. He's about to break open an RV camper door and bust the people inside. Unbeknownst to Hank, his brother-in-law, Walter White, a high school chemistry teacher turned crystal meth cook extraordinaire, is hiding on the other side of the camper door.

Desperate for a diversion, Walt orchestrates a phone call from Emergency Services to Hank. The Emergency Services dispatcher tells Hank his wife has been in a car accident and is being airlifted to the hospital. When Hank asks, "How is she?" the dispatcher dramatically states, "I wouldn't waste *any* time getting to the hospital."

Hank has an emotional hijack and goes into flight mode. He instantly forgets all about the impending drug bust, jumps in his Jeep, and speeds off to the Albuquerque hospital.[11]

Nearly thirty years ago, Daniel Goleman introduced the term amygdala (or emotional) hijack.[12] Despite its age, the concept is relevant now more than ever given pandemic-induced stress, fear, and burnout. So what happens in an amygdala hijack?

Research from Lieberman suggests an inverse relationship between activity in the amygdala and prefrontal cortex. When an emotional trigger takes place, the amygdala receives more blood flow and oxygen while the prefrontal cortex receives less. This causes the flight or fight response to kick in and rational thought to go offline.[13]

Hank's emotional trigger was learning that his wife had been in a car accident and was in the hospital. Shira's emotional trigger was being put on the spot about a deadline in front of the entire C-suite. These triggers shut down the outside world and turn the focus inward.

How do emotional hijacks prevent you from understanding others? They place your focus squarely on you. In this highly triggered state, you're not able to focus on others since your prefrontal cortex isn't fully online. Managing emotional hijacks is critical to self-control and regaining the ability to focus on others.

**your turn**

Describe a time you experienced an emotional hijack. How did it feel? How did it impact your ability to communicate and understand?

## what tools can you use to get better at understanding others?

Failing to listen, being an empathy miser, and emotional hijacking are three behaviors preventing understanding and keeping others from feeling understood. Here we will examine three tools to dismantle these barriers and move the needle on understanding.

### Listening

In this section, we'll explore the "three degrees of listening." These different depths of listening will help you enhance your listening capabilities. You will learn how to observe and detect spoken and nonverbal messages, which enhance understanding.

### *Degrees of Listening*

#### FIRST DEGREE: LISTENING TO SELF

The first degree of listening focuses more on you and less on the other person. You may hear the other person's words, but your attention is focused on yourself. You pay attention to *your* inner voice.

Random thoughts distract you as the other person speaks. You think to yourself, *Who's picking up the kids tonight? I forgot to buy that birthday gift for Mom's party! Where are we going this weekend?* Hearing someone else's words while you are listening to the running commentary in your head is possible because our brains process information about four times faster than we hear incoming words.[14]

**your turn**

Describe an instance where you used first-degree listening skills.

In summary, you're self-absorbed and listening to your own thoughts, opinions, judgments, feelings, and conclusions. Just like a first-degree burn impacts the epidermis or outer layer of skin, first-degree listening remains on a superficial level. Most conversation occurs at this first-degree level.

#### SECOND DEGREE: LISTENING TO OTHERS

The second degree of listening is directed at others rather than yourself. This active type of listening is laser-focused on the other person. It requires energy, presence, and attention.

Similar to a second-degree burn partially penetrating the dermis, second-degree listening digs a little deeper. To grasp more of the message, you search for, identify, and interpret various cues *from the other person.* These cues can be verbal, vocal, haptic (tactile), visual, or nonverbal.

The following table offers examples of each cue, describes each cue, and displays its associated percent of total message.

### communication cues

| cue | example (not exhaustive) | % of total message* |
|---|---|---|
| verbal | spoken words | 7% |
| vocal | voice tone and pitch, rate of speech, energy | 38% |
| nonverbal | gestures, facial expressions, body positions | 55% |

*dr. mehrabian's findings apply only when a person is communicating about an emotional or highly charged topic.

Take another look at the verbal percentage of the total message. Yes—7 percent—you read that right! Dr. Mehrabian's research suggests during emotion-laden communications, *we miss 93 percent of what someone is saying when we hear just their words!*[*15] How can this be? Like Hansel leaving a trail of breadcrumbs, there are multiple clues we can look for to help us find our way out of the dark forest.

Here's an example: you mention to your partner or spouse that you'd like to visit your parents this weekend. They say they'll be delighted to visit their in-laws, but they tell you this with a grimace on their face.

What do you detect about your partner's response? What did they say (or not say)? What cues or clues did you detect?

If you noticed:

Your partner's spoken words (*"delighted"* = *verbal cue*)

+ Your partner's facial expression (*"grimace"* = *nonverbal cue*)

= An inconsistent message

You earned a gold star!

*(For you overachievers, here's some extra credit. What did your partner not say? In other words, what nonverbal message did they send?)*

Behind each of these inconsistent messages is likely an emotional story waiting to be told. Darwin was the first to notice nonverbal messaging being used for emotional communications.[16] Decades later, Argyle's research found that people still prefer delivering emotional messages via *nonverbal cues* rather than words.[17] The next time you ask someone how they are, hear what they say *and* use your second-degree listening skills to listen for the unsaid.

◄ ◄ ◄   **pro tip**   ► ► ►

*When speaking with someone, observe their body language and facial expressions to translate unspoken messages.*

► ► ►   ▓   ◄ ◄ ◄

In summary, second-degree listening means that (1) you use your first-degree skills of hearing and listening to the other person's words; and (2) you connect vocal and nonverbal cues with words to understand the other person's dialogue, thoughts, and feelings. Just as in the partner case study here, *often it's what isn't said that is the true message.*

THIRD DEGREE: OMNIDIRECTIONAL LISTENING

The third degree of listening is the most active listening level. Listening at this degree uses your first- and second-degree listening skills *plus* your intuition, additional senses, and environmental awareness. It is called omnidirectional because your attention and focus is on you, on the other person, and on both of your surrounding environments.

To understand how listening at the third degree works, pretend you are playing the classic card game Concentration. To be effective at the game, you must match pairs of the same rank of card. Use the same principles here.

Hear the other person's words. Listen to their words and match them with the vocal and nonverbal cues. If they match, you have a pair!

If the words don't match the cues or something feels off to you, take a stab at what might be causing the mismatch. Observe the playing cards to track what's been turned over or what hasn't been touched. Use indicators in the surrounding environment to add important context to your intuition, guess, or hunch.

The table on the following page summarizes the Degrees of Listening tool.

How do listening and the Degrees of Listening tool counteract failing to listen?

When you listen with your brain, body, and intuition, you simply don't have the bandwidth to focus on how you would reply. You are busy interpreting signals from the other person and transmitting comprehension through multiple communication channels. This helps you listen at a deeper level to integrate

the other person's context, message, and intended meaning. This
also results in the other person feeling understood.

| degree of listening | your focus | action step(s) | senses involved | body parts engaged |
|---|---|---|---|---|
| first | self | • hear the other person's words<br>• focus on your own internal dialogue | hearing | ears, mind |
| second | other person | • hear the other person's words<br>• listen to what they say<br>• ask questions<br>• paraphrase what the other person says<br>• suspend your own internal dialogue<br>• identify vocal and nonverbal cues<br>• match cues with spoken words | hearing, vision | ears, mind, eyes, brain |
| third | self, other person, environment | • everything in second degree, plus these:<br>• listen for what they are not saying (words, vocal, and nonverbal cues)<br>• intuit or hunch what the (mis)alignment might represent using context<br>• sense the other person's energy, interest, attention, comfort, and trust levels<br>• assess surrounding environment's noises, smells, lighting, and temperature | hearing, vision, smell, sensation, intuition | ears, mind, eyes, brain, heart, gut |

◄ ◄ ◄  **pro tip**  ▶ ▶ ▶

*To determine which degree of listening is appropriate, pay attention to context. If you're ordering off a menu at a restaurant, then likely first-degree listening is sufficient. If you and your partner are fighting, first degree isn't the best choice. Second- or third-degree listening is more effective for leading or managing people.*

▶ ▶ ▶  ▦  ◄ ◄ ◄

The Degrees of Listening tool reflects a key competency of Human Leaders. *They understand others by listening with their senses, intuition, and brain.* As the skilled listener you are becoming, listen for verbal, vocal, and nonverbal cues, and discover any hidden or mismatched communications. Use the Degrees of Listening tool to expand your understanding capability.

**your turn**

Which two nonverbal cues will you keep an eye out for in your next conversation?

### Empathy

Ann is a leader in the insurance industry. Throughout her career, she's experienced at least one leader in every role who's "cut a bit differently."[18] With these leaders, Ann finds empathy helpful in understanding them.

Her empathy playbook starts with taking a step back from her assumptions about the person. She gets to know them. Her goal is to put herself in their shoes to understand their values and behavioral drivers. Most often, she finds a peer who is under an immense amount of pressure.

Ann says in her experience, some of the men with single-family income and family obligations tend to strongly prioritize ambition and self-preservation. This can lead to strong self-promotion and passive aggressive behavior to perceived threats or competition. She's learned that *when you understand what makes someone tick, it's easier to understand them.*

As a Human Leader, Ann uses a coaching mindset and approach to meet them where they are. She accepts their motivational drivers and doesn't judge them. She keeps her composure and poise and recognizes that it's not about her.

She is direct and upfront about desired outcomes. This helps the other person realize they are both on the same team with shared goals. When each side understands the other, Ann knows she'll realize a successful project.

Empathy is the act of putting yourself in someone else's shoes, like Ann did. Learning about other peoples' feelings, thoughts, and perspectives fosters your understanding of others. *Using empathy in your interactions with others helps you understand them AND helps them feel understood.*

### Emotional Self-Management

Have you heard of Capt. Chesley (Sully) Sullenberger? He's the highly experienced pilot who emergency landed a US Airways plane on New York City's Hudson River in 2009. Unbelievably, all 155 passengers survived the water landing.[19]

How did Sully accomplish this amazing feat? He managed his emotional temperature and kept his disruptive emotions in check. This allowed him to remain regulated and in control.

Staying regulated made it possible for him to keep his prefrontal cortex engaged and focused on the external environment.

The calm and poise Sully exhibited was due to decades of experience, training, and education in managing his emotions. Without this level of emotional self-control, there likely would have been a very different outcome to that emergency water landing. Sully's emotional self-management allowed him to understand what was going on around him and take immediate, considered action. Keeping calm under pressure is a critical tool in your Human Leader tool kit.

◄ ◄ ◄   **pro tip**   ► ► ►

*Sully's emotional self-management also contributed to keeping copilot Jeffrey Skiles and the flight crew calm.*

► ► ►  ▓  ◄ ◄ ◄

If you are a mercurial leader like Vishal Garg or stressed out due to deadlines like Shira, you might be prone to outbursts or angry comments when frustrated. If this happens to you, it may surprise you (like it did Shira). When you don't understand why an outburst happened and how to manage it, it can have devastating consequences for your life, leadership, career, and health, as well as for those around you.

*You cannot understand others unless you understand yourself.* Revisit Chapter 3 for tips on honoring and understanding the human you. Your ability to manage your own disruptive emotions is key to building self-understanding.

# what actions can you take to understand others?

To facilitate understanding of others, leaders can take several actions. This section discusses active listening and perspective taking. Let's look at each.

### Active Listening

Accenture's research suggests 96 percent of people wildly overestimate their listening skills.[20] The good news is, this means most people have no shortage of opportunities to be better listeners. To wit, research from Sullivan and Thompson suggests that 75 percent of us forget what we hear after just forty-eight hours.[21] Here are several tips to help you actively listen and understand others.

#### 1. Put Away Your Phone

Yes, really. Even better, put it on silent and flip it over. Optimally, turn it off. Sullivan and Thompson found that *even the possibility* of rings, pings, or dings diminishes cognition skills by 20 percent![22] No one likes to compete for your attention if you're texting, chatting, emailing, watching cat videos, or scrolling social media on your phone, and they shouldn't have to.

#### 2. Remove Distractions

Close doors or windows to block out ambient noise. Turn off the television or radio. Turn on "do not disturb" or "focus" mode on your phone or watch. Put a "do not disturb" sign on your office door. Turn off notifications on your laptop. If you are overwhelmed by visual input, turn off video on video calls or simply join audio-only.

### 3. Resist Multitasking

If you're on a conference or Zoom call, minimize your other browser windows. This will reduce the urge to check email or other multitasking attempts. Even more effective, close your email program or browser tab. These steps may even increase the quality of your work and relationships.

### 4. Engage with All Your Senses

Use eye contact to show you are paying attention to the other person. Listen with more than just your ears: use your senses, intuition, and awareness of the surrounding environment to listen to others. Include contextual knowledge to further shape your understanding of the other person's map of the world.

**your turn**

In which degree of listening do you spend the most time? Where would you like to spend most of your time? What do you need to shift to be an active listener?

If these suggested actions are too banal, or you find the degrees of listening too "woo-woo," that's fine. Let me be more blunt: to actively listen, close your mouth and stop talking. Give the other person your full attention. Open your ears and start listening.

### Perspective Taking

Joel Tauber is a retired CEO, philanthropist, and founder of the Tauber Institute for Global Operations at the University of Michigan. He has decades of experience leading and understanding others. Throughout his career, he's positively impacted thousands of lives through his leadership and philanthropic efforts.

He's learned it's critical to start with understanding what *people want*, rather than what others say is the right solution. Joel says, "You've got to go to the people to understand their problem."[23] For example, if you develop and implement a clean water solution for newly arrived Ethiopian refugees in Israel, but they really need to learn Hebrew so they can communicate in a foreign country, clean water isn't the most helpful solution.

To practice perspective taking, use your mind's eye to visualize two images: a person standing on an island and a person sitting in a boat.

Now add additional context. Imagine that one person is stranded on a desert island with a palm tree in the middle of the ocean, and the other person is lost at sea. What might each person be thinking and feeling?

The island dweller is likely suffering from loneliness and island fever and also delighted they're going to be rescued. The boater is probably seasick, dehydrated, and can't wait to set foot on land and drink some coconut water. Viewing the situation with context from two differing points of view reveals dramatically different interpretations, perspectives, and emotions.

Joel's collective impact approach to his philanthropic social change work is based on perspective taking. Human Leaders use perspective taking to "understand others by letting go of their point of view toward a situation to acquire the other person's mindset or point of view."[24] In other words, talk with people and *use their map of the world to understand what is important to them, what motivates them, and what they value.*

**Your Turn**

Practice perspective taking by watching Netflix and following
these six steps:

1. Tune into your favorite Netflix series, show, or movie that you
   can stop or pause.
2. Pause the show when the main character displays a strong
   emotion, such as anger, sadness, or joy, or is faced with a
   wrenching decision.
3. Grab a piece of paper or your e-device. Draw a stick figure to
   represent the main character and include a thought bubble
   above its head.
4. Jot down the main character's thoughts and feelings inside
   the thought bubble.
5. Note your thoughts and feelings about the scene in a
   separate bubble on the paper.
6. Compare these two points of view and note any similarities or
   differences.

### Building Emotional Intelligence (EI)

Research finds that 90 percent of the competencies differentiat-
ing star senior leader performers from the average are grounded
in EI.[25] Furthermore, Goleman suggests that EI is twice as
important as IQ and technical skills.[26] Therefore, building your
emotional intelligence can help you become a more effective
Human Leader.

Goleman offers four domains of emotional intelligence as a
starting point. These include self-awareness, self-management,

social awareness, and relationship management.[27] Human Leaders draw on their EI expertise to effectively lead themselves, others, and the business.

Feeling, recognizing, and naming your emotions are three actions you can take to expand your emotional vocabulary and build your emotional intelligence. This might sound simple, but it may not be easy! Brené Brown's research revealed most people have just a three-word vocabulary when it comes to labeling their emotions.[28]

**your turn**

Name the last five emotions you experienced.

◄ ◄ ◄  **pro tip**  ▶ ▶ ▶

*If your emotional vocabulary is limited to "happy," "sad," and "mad," you're not alone! Refer to Plutchik's Wheel of Emotions for a colorful, interactive visual depicting emotion vocabulary.[29]*

▶ ▶ ▶  ▦  ◄ ◄ ◄

## concluding thoughts

Research shows that we think only as much as we need to.[30] Our brains are wired to work efficiently and prefer shortcuts. These shortcuts impede understanding, as they are based on assumptions we make about someone given one or two facts that we already know.

Assumptions can negatively impact our understanding of others by limiting what we see. They shape how we interpret incoming information about others. In addition, they influence how we remember the information.

One way to counteract assumptions is to heed Lauraine Mulally's advice. She would tell her son Alan every day on his way to school, "It's more useful for you and everybody else that you seek to understand before you seek to be understood."[31] Bryce Hoffman, author of *American Icon: Alan Mulally and the Fight to Save Ford Motor Company*, recounts how Alan took that advice to heart:

> Mulally blew through the glass house like a Kansas cyclone, shaking hands, memorizing faces, and leaving everything changed in his wake. He would stop people in the hallway and ask them what they did and what they could do to improve the company. Instead of eating in Ford's famously posh executive dining room, he took his lunch in the company cafeteria. He stood in line with his plastic tray and chatted up accountants. He would sidle up to a table full of sales analysts and ask if he could join them. For Mulally, an open door was an invitation to pop his head in and see what was going on inside...[32]

Great leaders like Alan, Allie, Shira, and Gops Gopaluni, VP of Business Transformation Using Technology, prioritize understanding others. Gops advises that to create positive growth for everyone, "deeply understand the people you're working with. You'll become part of their success story just as they become part of yours."[33]

Gops's comment and Alan's example illustrate that *to be an effective Human Leader and drive results, you must understand people.*

Understanding people is one of the most critical tools you have as a human being and a Human Leader. The path to helping others feel understood starts with you.

# key takeaways

- The most basic of all human needs is to understand and be understood.
- It's easy to dehumanize people when you don't know them.
- It's important to pause and understand what others are really saying.
- Understanding others leads to effective communication, authentic relationships, and higher performance.
- When you listen with the intent to reply, you're no longer listening to someone else.
- Often, it's what is not said that is the true message.
- Human Leaders understand others by listening with their senses, intuition, and brain.
- Knowing what makes someone tick makes it easier to understand them.
- Interacting with empathy helps you understand others and helps them feel understood.
- You cannot understand others unless you understand yourself.
- To actively listen, close your mouth and stop talking. Open your ears and start listening.
- Human Leaders prioritize understanding people.
- Emotional intelligence helps you be a more effective Human Leader.

# HUMANS framework: mattering

## it mattered to brides: from one gown to hundreds

**m**eet Tricia.

Tricia Burger is a peppy, outgoing, and extremely successful New York Life agent and financial advisor. Tricia has dedicated her career to helping people protect what matters most to them—whether it's their wedding, their wealth, or their wishes. As the Detroit chapter president of the National Association of Women Sales Professionals (NAWSP), board member for Homes for Autism, and member of the Michigan

Business Travel Association, Tricia is known for helping people feel they matter.

In 1991, Tricia was planning her dream wedding and fell in love with a $1,600 wedding dress—twice the amount of her budget. To make up the deficit, she negotiated with the shop owner to work off the difference. She modeled bridal gowns for free, sold wedding dresses in the store, and in the process, learned a lot about the wedding industry.

Tricia married the love of her life in her gorgeous gown. However, she faced a big decision after her honeymoon. The bridal store owner wanted to retire and sell her the business. Tricia and her husband discussed it at length and ultimately decided to invest. Tricia recounts, "It's ironic that I walked in with a budget of $800 for one dress and essentially walked out with every gown in the store for $112,000 plus the business!"[1]

At that time, there were about ninety different bridal stores in Michigan. Each store had one sample dress in one size for customers to try on. If the bride decided to purchase the dress, the store would special order a gown for her.

The largest bridal shop around was called Boulevard Bridal in Birmingham, Michigan. If you were in the metro Detroit area, it was *the* place to buy your wedding gown. As the exclusive retailer for the coveted Bridal Originals brand, brides had placed 50 percent deposits on their special order dresses. Things were copacetic until Boulevard Bridal unexpectedly went out of business, causing chaos and stranding hundreds of brides without dresses for their weddings.

It was a huge scandal that made television and print headlines. Boulevard Bridal was broke—they weren't refunding any deposits for undelivered gowns and didn't pay the manufacturers. The brides were out their money with no gowns to show for it.

As a recent bride herself, Tricia understood the brides' fear and heartbreak about their dresses. As a bridal salon owner in her first year of operations, Tricia faced three significant challenges. She was the new kid on the block, brides had lost trust in bridal gown shops due to Boulevard Bridal, and the entire economy was in a downturn.

Tricia knew she had to act quickly or her business would go under before it even really got started. She called the Bridal Originals' sales representative. He told her they were in a quandary because they had dresses ready to ship but needed payment and a store to ship them to.

As a young entrepreneur with chutzpah, Tricia was used to thinking outside the box. She negotiated with him to pay for and take delivery of the hundreds of special order gowns for Boulevard Bridal. She then arranged to deliver brides their dresses, asking them to only pay their outstanding balance and offering to make alterations as needed.

It was a crazy amount of work since Tricia had no records from Boulevard Bridal. When the bride came in to pay for her dress, she had to trace the order back to the manufacturer, identify the delivery status, and locate the dress, which could be anywhere in the Midwest. Throughout the process, Tricia created a great partnership with Bridal Originals and a great relationship with brides, and word spread.

Tricia and her team became the heroes for distressed brides. The local TV stations picked up the story and featured her store in their reports. Tricia started delivering other manufacturers' gowns and became a bridal store of choice in the metro Detroit area.

Tricia made sure each bride got the dress of her dreams and felt beautiful in it, no matter what it took. In stark contrast to Boulevard Bridal's behaviors, *Tricia helped brides feel they were important and of significance*. Through Tricia's actions and behaviors, she demonstrated that the brides mattered as human beings, that it was about more than just dollars.

As a result, Tricia's business thrived. Within a year, she doubled operations and moved into a larger space. Her shop went from one of the smallest stores in the area to one of the top ten bridal salons in metro Detroit.

## what does it mean to matter?

Elliott defines mattering as "the perception that we are a significant part of the world around us."[2] To matter means that we are important and significant to others. We are valued for our contributions to the world as well as our humanity.

Tricia helped brides feel that they mattered by ensuring they had their bridal gowns in time for their weddings, one of the most important days of their lives. By making brides feel beautiful in the gowns of their dreams, Tricia helped these women feel cared for, important, and valued.

Eleonora Manuel is director of people operations, systems, and analytics at Outset Medical, Inc. When she came into the role, she launched an advanced data analytics business unit. Since the department is new, Eleonora prioritizes helping others understand how what she does matters and benefits the company. In Eleonora's words, "I'm the only person doing this, and people are really busy. They need to remember what I do and why it's important. This helps them see the value it adds to the organization."[3]

As a human being, Eleonora *herself* matters to Outset Medical's overall success. As a leader, she helps *others* matter through accurate forecasting, elevating diversity and inclusion efforts, and making Outset Medical an employer of choice for top talent. *Understanding how you matter helps you add value.*

Mattering is the third skill in the HUMANS framework.

**your turn**

How do you help others feel they matter?

## why is it important to matter?

To matter is a universal human need. When people don't feel they matter, they may also feel isolated, lonely, insignificant, rejected, or socially worthless. In extreme cases, it can lead to people committing unspeakable acts of violence.

Ethan Crumbley is a fifteen-year-old boy who allegedly executed a mass shooting at Oxford High School in Michigan in 2021. Four teens died, and many others were wounded. Shortly before the murders, he wrote on a piece of paper "my life is useless" and "the world is dead."[4] It's clear from these statements that Ethan didn't feel he mattered. Research on school shootings suggests that craving to matter yet feeling the opposite can have catastrophic consequences for society.[5]

In stark contrast, Amanda Gorman, the National Youth Poet Laureate who delivered US President Joe Biden's inaugural poem, shares how she learned *she* mattered. "I first knew my voice mattered when I recognized that I wasn't reading any voices like mine. That made me recognize the value of diversifying what I was hearing and experiencing, not just for myself but other young people out there."[6] *Amanda understood that how she could add value was to help others feel valued.*

Gallup reports employee engagement rates at a dismal 20 percent, costing the global economy $8.1 trillion in lost productivity each year.[7] Now more than ever, leaders must prioritize helping people matter. Simple ways to do this include managing workloads, communicating clearly, emphasizing well-being, and having employees' backs. It may seem trite, but it bears repeating: people don't care until they know how much you care.

"Everyone's important" is a core tenet of Alan Mulally's "Working Together" principles and practices. However, CEOs aren't the only ones who have high regard for mattering. Some countries do as well. France's national motto is "Liberté, égalité, fraternité." This means that each person is free, included, and equal, and each person belongs.

*Failing to feel valued can be construed as threatening our very essence of being.* Prilleltensky suggests that devaluing or overvaluing are "among the most serious threats facing society today."[8] People who feel excluded or that they don't matter may turn inward and become depressed or suicidal. In contrast, they may turn outward and join nationalistic movements led by authoritarian leaders in an effort to feel part of a broader community.[9]

The Arab Spring, Black Lives Matter, and LGBTQIA+ movements are examples of collective groups of oppressed people who have historically been devalued. DiAngelo notes *oppression is the opposite of mattering.*[10] Long overdue diversity, equity, and inclusion efforts are small steps on the long road to overcoming systemic racism and helping all people matter.

## what gets in the way of helping people feel they matter?

Leaders mentioned multiple behaviors getting in the way of helping people feel they matter. Passing judgment and prioritizing process over people topped the list.

### Passing Judgment

Have you ever heard of the Japanese aesthetic concept of "wabi-sabi"? Wabi-sabi is derived from the three existential Buddhist marks: imperfection, impermanence, and incompletion. In the field of art, "wabi-sabi" roughly translates to "flawed beauty" according to Koren.[11]

From the Japanese to the Navajo to the Persian, it is common to intentionally include a flaw in a finished art piece. This flaw is an example of wabi-sabi. The Japanese mend broken pottery with lines of gold, thereby highlighting the imperfections, while the Navajo weave rugs with a spirit line, "a single line of a contrasting color extending out from the center to the textile's edge."[12] Persian rug makers add their version of wabi-sabi by coloring one flower unique from the rest.

If you want a perfect piece of art, then neither the pottery nor the rugs will meet your requirements as each is flawed. It is the same with people. *Humans are wabi-sabi personified—each person is imperfectly perfect.*

By virtue of their humanness, people aren't perfect (although we expect them and ourselves to be!). Furthermore, we compare their actions, beliefs, and behaviors with our own, and when they differ from ours, we find them wabi-sabi and often judge them negatively.

This judgment rejects people as creative, resourceful, and whole human beings. Rejecting the person and judging their "imperfection" gets in the way of recognizing that they matter.

**your turn**

In which camp do you find yourself? Which camp do you help others join?

Not only does judging get in the way of helping people feel they matter, but it also creates two camps: "us" versus "them." The "us" camp is inclusive and fosters belonging. In contrast, the "them" camp is divisive and encourages separation.

### Prioritizing Process

Vauhini Telikapalli is the founder and CEO of VEVA, a professional strategy consulting firm. She was born in Vadodara, India, raised in Rochester Hills, Michigan, and currently resides in Baden, Switzerland.

Prior to becoming an entrepreneur, Vauhini moved to Switzerland to serve as commercial director for a brand-new business unit of a French company. As one of her performance goals, she was tasked to scale the unit from pre-revenue research and development to commercial operations. Knowing that performance was tied to results and the clock was ticking, Vauhini hit the ground running.

She aligned the team around a shared goal and assigned each member a performance target. Colorful sticky notes plastered the war room walls while easels reflected team members' handwriting from multiple brainstorming efforts. As a group, Vauhini and the team mapped out an aggressive roadmap with weekly, monthly, and quarterly milestones.

After several weeks, Vauhini recognized the team wasn't as engaged in their work. They were missing deadlines and milestones, placing the project in jeopardy. Moreover, she felt she and the team weren't connected, even though they had jointly created the plan. She tried talking with the team, but her efforts didn't seem to make any difference.

Vauhini decided to take the team out to dinner at a nice French restaurant in Zürich. She expressed her concerns to Pierre-Jean*, the French team lead. He told her, "You're not connected with us. It feels like our culture, who we are, and how we work don't matter to you. You're interacting with us like a typical American. All you seem to care about is the process and getting things done, no matter what the cost."[13]

Vauhini was stunned. She didn't realize her actions and behaviors made the team feel they didn't matter. She asked Pierre-Jean what she should do differently. He suggested that she do as the French do: slow down, have a glass of red wine, and connect as human beings first.

*Follow the principle of "when in Paris" here.
And even if you're not planning to live in France
or conduct business with the French, you'll
do well to heed Pierre-Jean's advice!*

► ► ► ▨ ◄ ◄ ◄

**your turn**

Where in your life
do you prioritize
process, tasks,
or things over
people?

Vauhini took Pierre-Jean's advice to heart. She immediately shifted how she interacted with the team to signal that they mattered to her. She decreased the laser focus on process and adopted a people-first approach. It wasn't long until things were back on track and the team delivered a successful project, on time and under budget.

## what tool can you use to help others feel they matter?

As I interviewed leaders about mattering, a pattern emerged. Leaders who made people feel valued exhibited similar behaviors. They inquired about accomplishments and aspirations. They sought to understand dreams and drivers. They leveraged strengths and spirit. They aligned employees' purpose with their work.

These outstanding leaders had higher levels of engagement on their teams, lower attrition rates, and overall improved performance. The MATTER model aggregates these leaders' actions into six executable steps.

*The MATTER model can also be used as part of the performance cycle or integrated into the onboarding process for new and experienced hires at all levels.*

▶ ▶ ▶ ▦ ◄ ◄ ◄

### MATTER Model

The MATTER model is a multidimensional framework for leaders at all levels to help others add value and feel valued. The six dimensions are Meaning, Accomplishments, Targets, Thinking, Energy, and Role.

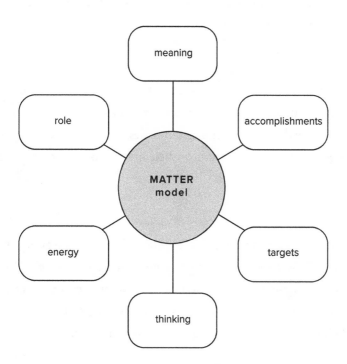

### Curate Meaning

Discover what motivates and drives each person. Identify their internal and external drivers. Elicit their why. Have them define their purpose or calling. Invite them to tell you how their drivers inspire their work.

### Celebrate Accomplishments

Gain awareness of each person's accomplishments. Understand how they got to where they are today. Seek out what the person is particularly proud of accomplishing and why. Identify what they had to overcome to realize these accomplishments. Most importantly, have them clarify how these accomplishments changed them or impacted their life for the better.

### Crystallize Targets

Learn where the person wants to go and what they want to achieve. Identify any support, resources, or knowledge required to achieve these goals. Pinpoint their desired timeframe for these targets. Have them share how their life will be different when they achieve these goals.

### Clarify Thinking

Gain clarity on the person's thinking preference—linear or conceptual. Determine what type of mindset they have—fixed or growth. Show interest in their perspective on a current organizational challenge. Explore how their thinking style influences their information processing and decision-making.

### *Craft Energy*

Evaluate what type of work expands or depletes each person's energy. Examine how you can create an energy-giving environment where they perform at their best. Tailor their work to what they love to do.

### *Create Role*

Ask each person to share their role and responsibilities at work. Have them identify to what extent they see themselves contributing to the greater good. Clarify one thing they would change about their work. Encourage them to explain how their role would be different if it was their dream job.

*Human Leaders love to help others add value and feel valued.* They achieve this by eliminating judgment and expanding understanding. Consider how you can integrate the powerful MATTER model into your Human Leadership tool kit to help others add value and feel they matter.

## what actions can you take to help others feel they matter?

Earlier, we touched on two ineffective behaviors preventing people from feeling they matter: passing judgment and prioritizing process. In this section, we'll address effective countermeasures: suspending judgment and prioritizing people.

### Suspend Judgment

My husband recently asked me, "How do you define 'being present'?" I responded, "I define being present as not being distracted."

My husband then said, "That's a reasonably good explanation." Intrigued that he assessed my comment *and* placed a value on it, I told him, "You're judging my definition."

We tend to place value judgments on other peoples' beliefs, thoughts, actions, or behaviors, often without realizing we're doing so. This value judgment comes from our own life experiences, religious dogma, values, beliefs, biological wiring, academic learning, and sports training. Value judgments tend to be "either/or" and take the form of good or bad, right or wrong, positive or negative.

To suspend judgment, bring an open mindset to the conversation. Notice when you begin to judge what someone says. Refrain from adding meaning to or making assumptions about what they say.

**your turn**

Pay attention to the next time you use "but" in a conversation. Then stop and consider what and whom you just judged or invalidated. How did it impact the other person?

◄ ◄ ◄   **pro tip**   ► ► ►

*When you begin a response with "but," be aware that you are judging. You are also simultaneously invalidating what the other person just said. When you invalidate someone's words, you also reject their worth.*

► ► ►   ▦   ◄ ◄ ◄

Accepting someone for who they are and what they say rather than judging them helps them feel they matter. This does *not* mean that you condone or agree with them. However, it *does* mean you intentionally set aside your own assumptions, beliefs, and mental models to understand how they contribute and add value to the world.

### Prioritize People

Franco Girimonte serves as the practice leader for North America HR Advisory at The Hackett Group. Prior to Hackett, Franco worked in Big Four consulting. One of his projects involved development and execution of a complicated finance functional strategy with an operating model.

Franco had a superstar on his team that another leader in the practice wanted. The superstar was plucked out of Franco's team, and a new team member dropped in her place. Franco heard through the grapevine the new person was just so-so. But Franco decided he would learn *what mattered to his new colleague*, how he could best support her, and what she might need to succeed.

Franco's plan was solid. First, he started with *tabula rasa*— Latin for "a clean slate." He suspended judgment about her past performance and viewed her as creative, resourceful, and whole. Second, he prioritized knowing her as a human being. He got to know her preferences, skills, and strengths and aligned work accordingly. Franco says, "She turned out to be remarkable. She was highly engaged, stayed on the project for eight months, had a great experience, and to this day, she's still working for the firm."[14]

Think of tabula rasa as the early Romans' version of an Etch A Sketch. You can write words or draw intricate pictures on it. But instead of shaking to erase it, you rub the slate with beeswax to remove any marks.

To achieve tabula rasa, you need an open mindset. How do you achieve an open mind? Look back at how Franco helped the new person on his team succeed. He set aside his assumptions. He intentionally opened his mindset to prioritize her as a person, rather than focus on the negative performance feedback he had heard about her.

Franco demonstrated he cared about her well-being and how she fared on the project. In turn, this new team member was highly engaged and contributed significant value to the team. This experience supports research from Towers Watson that shows "the single highest driver of engagement...is whether or not workers feel their managers are genuinely interested in their well-being."[15]

Tabula rasa helps others feel valued because it creates a

**your turn**

Where in your life could you leverage tabula rasa?

judgment-free zone. It enables you to accept people as they are. Unconditional acceptance helps people feel and perform at their best, contribute their unique value to the world, and matter to themselves, to others, at work, within society, and to the world.

## concluding thoughts

Christine Espinosa is a half-marathon runner, foodie, and world traveler with over thirty countries in her passport. She is currently a value engineer at Twilio Segment. Earlier in her career, she spent a summer interning at JPMorgan. As an intern, Christine didn't think she would get any face time with senior leaders. But the leadership of JPMorgan's asset and management division had other plans.

From day one, Christine was matched with two mentors. The CEO of asset management carved time out of his day to speak with the interns. In addition, the female CFO set up a lunch to talk with Christine and her fellow female interns about what it was like to be a woman in the financial services industry and workplace.

These outreach efforts positively impacted Christine and her career. She says, "Especially as an intern, it was a really great experience to have. Having senior leaders reach out and spend time with me showed me the value of a professional network. Building connections with people so high up in the organization showed me that even though I was an intern, I mattered to them."[16]

Prioritizing these interactions helped Christine gain exposure to people she may not have worked with otherwise. In addition, these relationships broadened and deepened Christine's network. And they ultimately furthered her career by opening the door to her role at Segment.

Like Alan at Ford, Indra Nooyi, former chairman and CEO of PepsiCo, prioritized building relationships with all employees: "You have to treat each person as though they are the most important person in that company."[17] As a leader, one of the most important things you can do is show people how much you value them.

Tarina understands this in spades. As a highly experienced people leader with many direct reports, Tarina (whom you met in Chapter 6) is specific about what she appreciates in her team members. She says, "People want to feel valued, need to feel *you value them, and know that their ideas are valuable.*"[18] In turn, her team members understand they are valued as human beings and for the specific contributions they bring to the table.

Indra, Tricia, Eleonora, Vauhini, Franco, Tarina, Alan, and the asset management leaders at JPMorgan understand the importance of helping people feel they matter. In its highest form, mattering "broadens individual and group capacity, leading to extraordinary outcomes" per Baker and Dutton[19] or "positive deviance," per Cameron, Dutton, and Quinn.[20] These leaders realize that *mattering is critical to building healthy, resilient, engaged, and high-performing organizations.*

*When what matters to others matters to you, you're on track to becoming a Human Leader.* Learning what matters to people creates understanding. Integrating what matters to people creates connection. Honoring what matters to people creates engagement and well-being.

# key takeaways

- To add value, help others feel valued.
- Leaders must prioritize helping people feel they matter.
- Feeling unvalued threatens our very essence.
- Oppression is the opposite of mattering.
- Humans are wabi-sabi works of art—imperfectly perfect.
- Human Leaders help others add value.
- Human Leaders help others feel valued.
- Mattering fosters engagement, connection, and community.
- Mattering creates healthy, resilient, and high-performing organizations.

# HUMANS framework: appreciating

## the aloha spirit: selfless appreciation

**m**eet Marilyn.

Prior to her retirement, Marilyn Asahi served as the humble, dynamic, and energetic principal of Kekaha Elementary School on the garden island of Kauai in the state of Hawaii. Marilyn was a dedicated, selfless principal—the kind who, if you have elementary school–age children, you wish was *your* kids' principal.

She cared deeply about students, taking money out of her own pocket to provide them food, shelter, and school supplies.

To Marilyn, making sure children can focus on learning and growing was mission-critical. Marilyn knows if a child doesn't have enough to eat or a roof over their head, they can't properly focus.

In Marilyn's view, she regarded the whole child as integral to the learning experience. This belief was reflected in Marilyn's vision for the *keiki* (kids) of Kekaha Elementary School: "All Pueo (owls) believe in their power to learn, grow, and own their future."[1]

Marilyn served the community throughout the COVID-19 pandemic by preparing and serving five hundred meals a day from the school's cafeteria to meet food security needs of students and local residents. She did this because serving others is second nature to her. Service to others is an integral part of Hawaiian culture. It is in Marilyn's DNA to help the broader community and support those in need.

During the pandemic months and immediately thereafter, Marilyn's teachers experienced significant change and uncertainty. They encountered stress unlike anything they'd ever experienced before. They modified lesson plans and learned how to teach virtually. They incorporated new operating model updates from the school district. Despite all of these stressors and uncertainty, the teachers put the kids first and ensured a high-quality learning experience for them.

In keeping with the aloha spirit, Marilyn sought to let her teachers and staff know how much she appreciated them and their hard work, long hours, and dedication. Marilyn created a staff and teacher appreciation wall of fame. She had professional headshots taken of each teacher. Below each headshot, she placed the teacher's name and a short biography highlighting their unique backgrounds and contributions.

When visitors, staff, students, parents, and teachers walk into the school office, the first thing they see is the appreciation board. It is prominently displayed on the wall.

*April 2021 Wall of Fame at Kekaha Elementary School. Image credit: Jozsef Bedocs.*

To Marilyn, leadership is similar to the Hawaiian principles of aloha. Aloha means respecting and selflessly caring for others without expecting it in return.[2] Aloha is a way of life, deeply ingrained in Marilyn's spirit, heart, and beliefs. Marilyn is a true aloha leader. As someone who prioritizes appreciating others, puts people first, and doesn't seek accolades, fame, or fortune for herself, Marilyn reflects Human Leadership at its best.

## how do you define appreciating others?

Merriam-Webster defines appreciation as "a feeling or expression of admiration, approval, or gratitude." Examples include thanking an employee for doing stellar work, hugging a spouse to acknowledge their meal preparation, or showering a child with praise for sharing their toys.

Research suggests that gratitude has two components: (1) recognizing a positive benefit and (2) recognizing the benefit's source.[3] In the same vein, *appreciation involves recognizing and thanking others for generating positive outcomes.*

Throughout 2020 and 2021, communities publicly thanked healthcare workers and first responders for their heroic efforts. These demonstrations of appreciation showed up in different ways. People clapped from apartment windows in New York City, lined subdivision streets in mid-America to welcome heroes home after long shifts, and hosted cheerful parades in New England to celebrate them.[4]

**your turn**

What do you do to appreciate others? How do you help people feel appreciated?

Marilyn helped teachers and staff feel appreciated by thanking them for their outstanding efforts through a publicly displayed wall of fame.

Appreciating is the fourth skill in the HUMANS framework.

## why is it important to appreciate others?

Simply put, it feels good to appreciate others. It also lifts others up and helps *them* feel good about themselves. It creates positive emotions and heightens relational energy.

However, appreciating others isn't just a feel-good activity. Employees who feel appreciated and valued stay with their employers. This decreases flight risk and attrition costs, which can run tens of thousands of dollars per employee.

Adam Grant's research finds that employees who feel appreciated and are shown gratitude from leaders realize 50 percent productivity gains.[5] In contrast, the Swedish WOLF study suggests employees (especially male) whose bosses don't appreciate them are *at 50 percent greater risk for heart attacks and disease.*[6] Mic drop. Read that again and let it fully sink in. In other words, *employee health and well-being are linked to leadership's ability to appreciate others.*

While teaching organizational behavior at the University of Michigan, I had students self-select into teams in the first class. After working together the entire semester, I asked students to jot down what they appreciated about their team members during the last class. There was lots of laughter and animated conversation—and even a few tears—as students shared their notes of appreciation with each other.

The lower-performing teams finished quickly, while higher-performing teams took more time to share their comments. After speaking with each team, I discovered the high-performers had written down more appreciative comments about each other.

This aligns with research findings that high-performance teams express more instances of positive feedback than do low-performing teams.[7]

Expressing gratitude creates oxytocin—the social glue that promotes bonding. Therefore, *the more people feel appreciated, the more they bond and engage in their work and with others.* Increased engagement elevates relationships and work performance. Appreciating others and helping them feel appreciated *creates virtuous cycles of performance and engagement,* which are critical to individual well-being and organizational survival.

## what behaviors get in the way of helping people feel appreciated?

My research with top leaders reflects two key behaviors that act as barriers to helping others feel appreciated: withholding gratitude and taking credit for others' work. Let's look at each one.

### Withholding Gratitude

Research shows that 81 percent of employees would work harder if their bosses demonstrated gratitude toward them. However, people are less likely to show gratitude at work than any other place, despite advantages thereof.[8] If gratitude is such a game changer, and employees really feel it's important, then why isn't it more prevalent in the workplace? Why don't more leaders express appreciation?

Multiple factors seem to play a role in withholding gratitude. For leaders, some feel it is unnecessary, believing that salary or pay should be thanks enough. Fear of being vulnerable or taken advantage of also factors into why bosses withhold demonstrating appreciation. Other leaders, particularly those with a command-and-control mindset, view it as coddling employees. For leaders unaccustomed to thanking others, it may come off as forced, awkward, or just plain fake.

Remember Bill Lumbergh, the company vice president in the 1999 movie *Office Space*? He asks employee Milton to move his office to the basement. Milton, despite his reservations, complies. As Bill walks away from Milton's new basement office location, he half turns around and tells him: "*Thanks a bunch, Milton.*"[9] Although Bill's comment insinuates appreciation, his body language, tone of voice, and tonality of speech ooze insincerity and reflect the chasm between his spoken words and intended meaning.

On the other hand, some employees (and leaders) choose to demonstrate insincere gratitude simply to advance their own agenda. You know the ones I am talking about—they're the brownnosers who suck up to the boss for the coveted stretch assignment, promotion, day off with pay, or cushy office. *Expressing inauthentic gratitude is just as damaging as withholding authentic appreciation—perhaps even more so.*

The harmful effects of failing to appreciate others in the workplace create a falling domino effect. In 2021, nearly *48 million employees* left their jobs, generating one of the largest talent shifts in history.[10] When employees don't feel appreciated, they leave. In other words, *not feeling appreciated creates attrition.*

**your turn**

From whom do you withhold gratitude? Why?

### Taking Credit for Others' Ideas, Contributions, Work

Throughout my career, I pulled many all-nighters to get presentations done for the next morning's meeting. Then, during the meeting, instead of me presenting my own work, a male peer or boss presented it *and* took credit for the contributions instead. Frequently, I wasn't acknowledged for the ideas, work, or effort. I didn't feel appreciated and joined those organizations' alumni ranks soon thereafter.

Peers, colleagues, or superiors claiming credit for your work truly sucks. It's one of the quickest ways to destroy rapport, relationships, and trust. As a leader, it's also an effective way to get yourself blackballed by colleagues, or to be included on the informal list of "do-not-work-for-leaders," when employees discuss potential moves at the watercooler or happy hours.

With so much else going on in the world, why does this persist in today's workplace? To be fair, taking credit *can be* an honest mistake. However, in my experience and per all of the leaders I interviewed, it's more often related to power and control in the kingdom, knowledge hoarding, needing to add value, or a lack of self-confidence on the credit taker's part.

**your turn**

How often do you take credit for someone else's work?

Why does this stop others from feeling appreciated? Because the receiver of appreciation isn't the other person: it's your own ego. *Taking credit for others' work prevents you from acknowledging someone else's contributions to the greater good. Worse, it diminishes them as a human being.*

## what tools can you use to get better at helping others feel appreciated?

My dad, Bob, loves watching YouTube to learn how to fix stuff. Being hands on and a big DIYer, he's also a huge fan of tape— duct tape, painter's tape, masking tape—you get the idea. When I bought my first house, he gave me two six-packs—one each of silver duct and tan masking tape—and told me, *"There isn't anything you can't fix with duct tape."* With a 1960s house that seemed to be a DIY original, over the years, I learned there was a small element of truth to this.

However, my dad had one other favorite (albeit conflicting) piece of advice. *"You need the right tool for the job to do the job right."* Figuring out when to use tape versus a different tool in my toolbox for my old, jerry-rigged house was, at times, overwhelming.

Appreciation is the same way. There are many tools you can use to help others feel appreciated. Determining which is best may seem daunting but here are three simple steps you can take to appreciate others with confidence, clarity, and finesse.

- First—Learn what makes each person feel appreciated
- Second—Gather any needed resources
- Third—Appreciate others *how they prefer to be appreciated*

In other words, taking a few moments to invest in someone helps others feel appreciated. *Showing appreciation doesn't require a lot of time, money, or effort.* Yet it reaps enhanced performance, stronger relationships, and increased engagement.

## what actions can you take to help others feel appreciated?

Leaders I interviewed shared the following actions as part of their appreciation repertoire.

▪ Ken*, a biotechnology director, publicly appreciates his team: "I demonstrate appreciation during virtual town halls by giving a shout-out to my team. I share their accomplishments and extra efforts to meet deadlines and deliver value for the organization."

▪ Remember Shira from Chapter 7? She highlights the importance of consistently and authentically thanking others: "I walk around the office to thank people one-on-one. I'm really big on expressing gratitude."[11]

▪ Brad from Chapter 6 shows how appreciation takes place in the military: "My commanding officer made it his mission to get to as many people on the ship as he could. Over two weeks, he had to have gotten to damn near every single person, shaking their hand and saying, 'Hey, I appreciate what you're doing.'"[12]

▪ Damian (coming up in Chapter 12) shares how as a CFO he appreciated his colleagues: "My colleague's job was different from mine, but he put a lot of effort and care into it. I really appreciated the fact that he did that. I would occasionally stop and tell him that because no one else did. Throughout my career in different organizations, I observed some people willing to make that investment and others who weren't."[13]

- Tracy McCrea, a sales executive with Windsor Jewelers, applies the platinum rule to her appreciation efforts. Leveraging her knowledge of her clients' unique preferences, she curates a bespoke appreciation experience. From bottles of champagne to fine dining to special outings, Tracy ensures the experience is meaningful, emotionally moving, and memorable.

Savvy leaders like Ken*, Shira, Brad, Damian, and Tracy understand that demonstrating appreciation is a powerful leadership strategy. *Appreciating others how they want to be appreciated honors their humanity.* Furthermore, it also appreciates the bottom line.

**your turn**

Life is short. Appreciate someone today.

### Thank Others

Rare in today's digital world, thank-you notes are a lost art. They not only differentiate you from everyone else sending an email or a text, but they also have a more personal, intimate touch. When was the last time you received a handwritten thank-you note?

My best friend's son, Samuel, is an aspiring artist and talented drummer. In December 2021, he sent me a handwritten thank-you note. Samuel took the time to design, draw, and decorate the card, print and cut it out, assemble it, and then handwrite a personal note. This meant a lot to me, and it has a place of honor on the refrigerator.

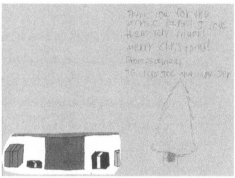

Thank-you notes aren't just limited to home life. O'Flaherty suggests that *handwritten notes can boost workplace motivation*, particularly when they are personalized.[14] The key is to be sincere and authentic with the message.

Although handwritten notes may be a lost art for many, it's a practice that is alive and well for exemplary Human Leaders. CEO Sheldon Yellen handwrites cards each week for employees—nearly 9,200 a year.[15] Douglas Conant, former president and CEO of the Campbell Soup Company, wrote thirty thousand thank-you notes in ten years.[16] Former chairwoman and CEO of PepsiCo Indra Nooyi had a unique twist for her thank-you notes.

Instead of writing to employees, she wrote hundreds of thank-you notes to *their parents*. In these letters, Indra thanked them for their adult child and the positive contributions they made to the world and to PepsiCo. As Indra comments, "Parents were over-joyed to get a report card about their child at any age."[17]

It's been thirteen years since I received that handwrit-ten thank-you note (see Introduction) from former president and CEO of Ford Motor Company Alan Mulally. The impact was so strong, it led me to write this book. Human Leaders like Sheldon, Douglas, Indra, and Alan recognize the magic, long-lasting, and transformative power of a personal, handwrit-ten thank-you note.

Demonstrating appreciation isn't just limited to thank-you notes. During the pandemic, leaders showed appreciation in var-ious ways. Employees received everything from company-logo T-shirts, fitness gear, BPA-free water bottles, and hats, to meal delivery service and home office decor staples such as clocks, pens, and coffee mugs.

Other tools to demonstrate gratitude include sending healthy fruit or beautiful flower arrangements, buying someone a coffee or a gift card to their favorite restaurant, or simply telling them thank you in person and specifying what it is you appreciate.

In summary, demonstrating appreciation manifests in a vari-ety of ways. As a best practice, check in with someone to learn what form of appreciation they prefer. For example, some may be comfortable with public praise or an article published in the company newsletter, while others may prefer something more private, such as a one-on-one coffee, a handshake, or a written thank-you note.

**your turn**

To whom will you write a handwritten thank-you note today?

## concluding thoughts

With technology continuing to influence how, where, and with whom we work, it's more important than ever to appreciate humans. Dr. Jess Evans is an information technology executive. Jess shares her perspective on how appreciation contributes to effective human interaction: "Leaders must recognize that every human is different. When they appreciate those differences, that's when they build mutually beneficial and successful relationships."[18] Honoring each person's uniqueness reflects appreciation at a human level.

Damian G. Zikakis, executive coach and CliftonStrengths trainer at DGZ Coaching, offers his insights on appreciation: "My biggest insight is that people are really willing to go the extra mile when they are appreciated for their strengths and accommodated."[19] In his work, Damian has observed that even small efforts from leaders result in large employee performance gains.

As the Human Leaders throughout this chapter demonstrate, appreciation is the roadmap to unleashing human potential. It takes mere seconds and costs nothing. It's available to everyone. Best of all, it honors people where it matters most—at the core of their humanness. Being appreciated is key to the human experience.

# key takeaways

- To appreciate others, acknowledge and thank them for their positive contributions.
- Feeling appreciated augments employee well-being.
- Failing to appreciate employees negatively impacts their health.
- The more people feel appreciated, the more they bond and engage.
- Leaders who appreciate others create virtuous performance cycles.
- Expressing inauthentic gratitude is just as damaging as withholding authentic appreciation.
- Employees who don't feel appreciated leave.
- Taking credit for others' work diminishes them as human beings.
- Showing appreciation doesn't require a lot of time, money, or effort.
- Appreciating others how they want to be appreciated honors their humanity.
- Honoring each person's uniqueness reflects appreciation at a human level.
- Appreciation is the roadmap to unleashing human potential.
- Feeling appreciated is key to the human experience.

# 10

# HUMANS framework: iNspiring

## handshakes help turn around a toxic culture

**m**eet Brad.

Brad Brezinski is an avid trail runner, red wine enthusiast, and aspiring guitarist who founded the consulting think tank S2A. Prior to his entrepreneurial venture, Brad held the role of CFO of General Tool Company, a defense contractor based in Cincinnati, Ohio. Brad also is a retired Navy officer, having served for over two decades in active duty and reserve capacities.

During Brad's Navy days, he received orders to go to an air-craft carrier dry-docked in Norfolk, Virginia. When he arrived, there were two months left in the maintenance project, and it was severely behind schedule. The ship's commanding officer had declared lockshift.

Lockshift requires twelve-hour shifts seven days a week, in addition to regular duty every three days. Therefore, in a seven-day week, crew members would work five twelve-hour days and two twenty-four-hour days. Brad explains, "Lockshift normally wouldn't last for more than a week—it's brutal and not done unless absolutely necessary."[1] But when Brad arrived, the commanding officer had already had the crew in lockshift for three weeks.

Brad recalls, "When I stepped on board, the culture was completely toxic. Every conversation was awful. You could feel the heaviness and see the stress in everybody's eyes. I hadn't experienced anything like it before, and I've never seen anything like it since." Then several tragic events occurred, which attracted senior leadership's attention.

Senior leadership personnel performed a climate assessment with abysmal results. After discovering that the lockshift had been going on for three weeks, the commanding officer was fired. A new commanding officer was assigned to the 3,500-person air-craft carrier.

The new commander immediately stopped the lockshift and put everyone on a three-day stand-down. He didn't make any other policy or culture changes in his first few weeks. He simply walked around and tried to meet as many people as he could one-on-one or in small groups.

When he met with people, he'd say, "Hey, I appreciate what you're doing. I'm looking to make some changes on the ship, and I'd love to hear your feedback on what you think could be better." Then he went back to Washington, DC for a week to create his initial assessment report.

When the commander returned to the ship, he called a one-on-one meeting with each of his twelve direct reports. In each meeting, the commander shared an inspiring vision about the aircraft carrier's new culture. He framed it from the perspective of someone who had never seen the ship before and was stepping on board for the first time. He described what the person would see, how they would be greeted, how crew would interact with each other as well as guests, how they would respect their spaces and keep them immaculately clean, and how they would approach their work.

After the commander finished telling the story, he told each direct report, "This is where we're going to be in six months. First, I need to know that you will support this vision. Second, I need you to hold everyone under your charge to this standard." He would look each person in the eye, and if someone couldn't do either of those two things, he told them to leave the ship.

Out of his twelve direct reports, four left. Of the eight who stayed, he told them, "Now, I want you to meet with your direct reports and have them meet with theirs as well. I expect within seventy-two hours we've reached every single person on the ship."

Many crew members left over the three-day period. After ferreting out the toxicity, the commander ensured that everyone was exhibiting the new vision's values daily. If there was an issue, the commander would pull the person aside and call them out on it.

One day, the commanding officer asked to meet with Brad from 14:15 to 14:20. Brad was excited to meet with him, because he liked the commander and held him in high regard. At the appointed time, Brad went up to the commander's office anticipating a great conversation.

Brad got his ass chewed instead. The commander had observed one of Brad's direct reports publicly dressing down a subordinate in the mess hall. He said, "That is inconsistent with the way we should be treating one another. I expect you to fix it."

Brad replied with the only correct answer available: "Yes, sir." Then he left the office to fix the problem.

Shortly thereafter, Brad left the ship for a new post. As he walked off the ship for the last time, he noticed stark differences between the past and present. The atmosphere was light and people respected each other and took pride in keeping their workspaces immaculate. The negative toxicity, heavy atmosphere, and brutal lockshift were but distant memories.


## what does it mean to iNspire?

Inspire stems from the latin word *inspirare*, meaning "to breathe into." The act of inhaling moves the lungs and sends oxygenated blood coursing throughout the body. Like breathing in, a leader's *inspiration creates direction and shapes movement* of follower efforts toward a desired outcome.

To *inspire others propels them to act of their own accord.* The crew members believed in their commander's inspirational vision. They verbally committed to embody the vision's values. They held each other accountable to that vision. They did this not because they were told to but because they *chose* to. *Inspiration facilitates agency.*

Effective leaders inspire others to greatness. Inspiring others creates momentum toward a desired outcome. In a nutshell, *inspiration results in getting results.*

iNspiring is the fifth skill in the HUMANS framework.

**your turn**

How do you iNspire others?

## why is it important to iNspire others?

In the 1970 movie *Patton*, the opening scene shows Gen. George S. Patton standing in front of a gigantic American flag. The camera pans over him, highlighting several artifacts of his success: a chest full of shiny medals, an engraved white-handled pistol, and four gold stars on his helmet reflecting his rank of general.

Patton rallies the troops before sending them into war. He paints a clear vision of how they will win against the enemy. He proclaims how "real Americans" love to fight, love a winner, and will not tolerate losers.

He touts how he has the best men in the world in his army. He brazenly assures them that "they won't chicken out and will do their duty." He has them visualize how they'll tell war stories to their grandsons while sitting in front of fireplaces. He tells them he'll be "proud to lead their wonderful selves into battle anywhere."[2]

*Inspiration is important because it creates pictures of possibility.* Without it, things remain status quo or even stuck. There may have been a different end to World War II, for example. One that wasn't in favor of the Allies. One that didn't inspire soldiers to willingly go to the front line and risk their lives.

Patton's pragmatic yet intense delivery of his message worked, because he was authentic. If he had been otherwise, the troops wouldn't have responded so favorably. *Inspiration combined with authenticity begets followership.*

## what behaviors get in the way of iNspiring others?

During my research, four behaviors hindering inspiration came to the fore. Lack of vision, inability to tell stories, inauthentic leadership, and lack of trust consistently showed up as inspiration killers.

### Lack of Vision

What do Borders, Kodak, and Blockbuster all have in common? They each lacked leadership with vision that strategically adapted to changing market conditions. Working for leaders without vision is like driving at night without headlights—it's dark, hard to see, and easy to drive off a cliff.

Without vision, there is no goal. Without a goal, leaders have nothing to direct people toward. *Visionary leaders create goals that inspire people to collaborate toward a common end.*

**your turn**

Describe a time when you worked for a leader without vision.

Multiple researchers' work suggests *visionary leaders are more effective than those lacking vision.*[3] But all is not lost. Developing vision is a key leadership skill that can be learned.

### Inability to Tell Stories

Captivating storytellers are few and far between. When they are your professor, it's even more memorable. During one of my Michigan MBA strategy courses, Professor Gautam Ahuja shared a tragic story with a heart-wrenching ending.

Union Carbide operated a pesticide plant in Bhopal, India. On December 2, 1984, tons of methyl isocyanate and other toxic gasses accidentally leaked into the air, killing thousands of employees and local residents and causing severe injury to hundreds of thousands of human beings. *The New York Times* called it the worst industrial disaster in history.[4]

In 1989, India's Supreme Court ordered Union Carbide to pay $470 million to victims and the injured.[5] Twenty-four years later, 554,895 people had received compensation for their injuries.[6] The families of the 15,310 killed each received just $2,200 on average.[7]

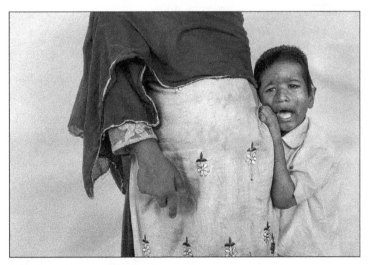

*Photo Copyright Judah Passow©8*

In 2022, nearly forty years later, tons of hazardous waste remain buried underground, contaminating groundwater. Survivors are still fighting with the plant's current owner, Dow Chemical, to clean it up. Many women exposed to the gasses as children have grown up and given birth to children with physical defects or mental conditions, requiring ongoing medical care.[9]

Twelve years after graduating, I still remember Professor Ahuja delivering this story as part of his class lecture. I was heartbroken by the accident's devastating consequences on employees and the local population. Further, I was appalled by the low dollar value placed on a human life.

**your turn**

Which captures your attention more—a story or a statement?

Memorable stories capture our attention, pull on our heartstrings, and inspire us to action. *Stories are in our DNA—they're how we learn, love, and live.* Leaders who can't tell stories miss powerful opportunities to be memorable, inspirational, and followable.

### Inauthentic Leadership

Amy Anger is a shameless extrovert, realistic optimist, and founder of Atrip Consulting. Early in her corporate career, Amy got a promotion and ended up reporting to a "keeping people at arm's length," corporate-veneer type of leader. His style was to hold things close to his chest, reveal nothing to direct reports, and be exceptionally formal.

A few days into her new role, Amy received feedback saying she needed to tone down her authentic self. She was told she must grow executive presence. She needed to fit the mold of what executives in the company should look, speak, and act like. So she changed her behavior.

Amy stopped being transparent with her team and shared less. She made fewer jokes and was more serious. She ensured everyone observed her working hard and having less fun.

In turn, Amy's team, who had reported to her for over ten years, struggled with this new Amy. They didn't recognize the buttoned-up, guarded, and serious executive standing in front of them. To make matters worse, they didn't know or understand her anymore and lost trust in her.

It wasn't just Amy's direct reports who struggled. Amy, too, rumbled with this new version of herself. In Amy's words, "I was a version of me that I didn't know. It felt like I was wearing a costume."[10] Wearing this particular executive persona did not come naturally to her.

However, Amy kept trying to make it work. To justify persisting, she told herself she couldn't rely on what got her to this point to make her successful going forward. She believed she needed to shift who she was and change her behaviors to be successful in the new executive role.

It didn't take Amy long to realize her inauthentic leadership style simply didn't work—for her or her team. As Amy says, "If you're trying to be someone you're not, it just makes leading a team that much harder because they can't connect to or trust you." Ultimately, after much deliberation, Amy chose to step away from the role and return to her authentic self.

**your turn**

When have you been like Amy and worn "a costume" that didn't feel right?

Amy's story demonstrates that leading inauthentically destroys trust. It creates uncertainty and behavioral inconsistency. In short, *inauthentic leadership inhibits inspiration.*

### Lack of Trust

Rotter defines trust as an expectation of an individual or group that their word, promise, or verbal or written statement is reliable.[11] Choosing to trust another human being is an intentional action. We can choose to grant trust, or we can opt out.

◄ ◄ ◄　**pro tip**　► ► ►

*Whether trust is given upfront or withheld until earned directly correlates with organizational performance.*

► ► ►　▓　◄ ◄ ◄

Research demonstrates that in organizations with high trust levels, performance *exceeds that of low-trust organizations by 286 percent* when considering stock price plus dividends.[12] Furthermore, companies on the "Great Places to Work List" outperform the market by 288 percent, a three to one ratio![13] It's clear from these examples that trust is a performance multiplier. Why, then, is trust so elusive at work?

Inauthentic leadership may be one reason, as we saw from Amy's story. People sense when leaders aren't being their authentic selves. Hugh from Chapter 4 elaborates: "You've got to be real. People have a built-in BS meter, and they'll say, 'He's saying the right words, but they just don't land. I can't put my finger on it, but something doesn't feel right.' The BS detector tells them something is off and trust is withheld."[14]

Unwritten cultural rules dictating workplace behavior are a second reason. These norms insinuate that trust must be earned first, rather than given. When this happens, it sends a harmful and often hurtful message. It implies simultaneously that colleagues are neither worthy of trust nor reliable. *Inspiration and distrust cannot coexist—the two are mutually exclusive.*

Thirdly, those who trust first may be perceived as weak. In some cases, those who trust first get burned, taken advantage of, or screwed over by people with positional power. For the trusting party, this perpetuates distrust going forward, withdrawal from the organization's social fabric, and even attrition. In worst-case scenarios, it engenders additional bullying or leads to retaliatory actions, causing lack of psychological safety and mental health issues. The absence of trust hurts human beings, harms relationships, and hinders performance.

**your turn**

Do you trust first, or do you make others earn your trust? Why?

## what tools can you use to get better at iNspiring others?

We've looked at four barriers that inhibit being inspirational and inspiring others. Now let's review four tools to help eliminate these blockades.

### Vision Crafting

Crafting vision is an essential Human Leadership skill. *Without vision, it's impossible to inspire others. Despite its importance, many organizations struggle under leaders lacking vision.*

Fewer than 0.1 percent of leaders have a vision, per Dr. Oleg Konovalov's research.[15] Leaders commonly lack vision because they are unaware of the need for it and do not possess the necessary skills for creating and executing it.

To create a compelling vision, you have to be able to see the future in ways other people can't. Konovalov describes six required elements of crafting a compelling vision: clarity, ability, viability, influence, action, and revitalization. When these elements are present, a desired future becomes more real. Konovalov elaborates: "Vision is aspiration for the future that we strive to make a reality today."[16]

Vision acts as a magnet, drawing people toward a desired future. Konovalov explains: "We reach minds by communicating vision. We reach hearts and souls by sharing it."[17] In this way, *vision creates relational connections and inspires people at the heart and mind levels.*

### Storytelling

To address cultural issues, Brad's commander told stories. Instead of barking out orders upon his return to the ship, he painted a vision of the future state: a story about what it would look, feel, and sound like to be the greatest aircraft carrier in the Atlantic fleet. This radically changed the aircraft carrier's culture within ninety days—an impressive feat. His story enabled the 3,500-person crew to connect to an aspirational future, internalize it, and make it real.

Leaders who are effective storytellers include three key elements in every story: setting the stage, creating a conflict, and delivering a resolution. These elements make the story personal, create a hook, and resolve the tension. Watch a TED talk or listen to *The Moth Radio Hour* to catch this framework in action.[18]

This three-element approach is key to effective storytelling, says Jonah Sachs.[19] Because it's in our DNA to create, communicate, and consume stories, they are how we learn and engage best. Stories with an emotional tug on the heartstrings are "sticky," which makes them memorable and spurs action. *Human Leaders inspire others to action through storytelling.*

### Authentic Leadership Questionnaire

The Authentic Leadership Questionnaire (ALQ) is an empirical, quantitative tool developed by Walumbwa.[20] It consists of sixteen questions on four dimensions measuring self-awareness, relational transparency, morals and ethics, and balanced processing.

There are two versions: one for leaders to self-assess and another for employees to rate their leaders. The questionnaire is available in both free and fee-based versions.[21] As a multi-rater, or 360 performance assessment, this is a reliable and evidence-based tool to assess perceptual differences of your leadership between you and your stakeholders.

The first dimension, self-awareness, asks the leader to rate the extent to which they are aware of their own strengths, weaknesses, others' perceptions of them, and their impact on others. Balanced processing explores how the leader solicits others' perspectives and viewpoints for consideration when making decisions. The moral and ethical conduct questions seek to understand which morals and values guide the leader's beliefs and behaviors. Lastly, relational transparency strives to determine the leader's environmental aesthetic, so that others may feel safe sharing ideas, content, or challenges.

Being clear about your leadership behaviors and how others perceive you impacts your ability to inspire others. As Amy found out, when you're not your authentic self, people can tell you're faking it, and they won't follow you. *Leaders who are their authentic selves inspire others.*

### Trust Equation

The Trust Equation is a quantitative instrument featured in *The Trusted Advisor*. It includes twenty questions based on the four factors of trust: credibility, reliability, intimacy, and self-orientation. Respondents receive an individual report indicating their overall Trust Quotient (TQ) score, individual factor scores, and preferences for building trust.[22]

The credibility factor explores words, skills, credentials, and others' perceptions of expertise. Reliability relates to actions, predictability, and dependability. Intimacy involves how safe people feel in sharing confidences. Self-orientation refers to external versus internal focus. The free version of the instrument includes a limited report.[23]

If trusting others doesn't come easily to you, or if others doubt your trustworthiness, it's difficult at best to inspire others. *Leaning into, instead of away from, trust expands relationships, human connection, and business results.* Trusting others and improving your trustworthiness are key to building your inspiration muscle.

## what actions can you take to iNspire others?

As an integral part of their leadership repertoire, Human Leaders breathe inspiration into the organization's culture. Below are four specific actions to liven up your leadership and be inspirational.

### Create Vision

Gops Gopaluni is vice president of Business Transformation Using Technology at a large professional services firm. In this role, Gops manages globally distributed teams of up to 150 people on complex client engagements. He is consistently recognized for client engagement excellence. These results stem from his expertise at putting people first and crafting vision.

To create an energizing vision, Gops engages his team members. He invites them to shift their mindsets. He proposes they consider themselves CEO of their domain, regardless of task or role. For example, even if they're answering phone calls at the front desk, he still wants them to think of themselves as the CEO of phone calls.

Gops then takes it one step further. He paints a clear picture of the future. In this aspirational future, team members have autonomy, accountability, and agency. Gops explains, "As the CEO, I want you to own everything that happens there. If you ever run into problems, I'm here to support you and help find solutions. I want you to be empowered to be a great CEO in what you do."[24]

As a result, team members go above and beyond because they feel supported as individuals and human beings, rather than employees assigned to a task. Gops likens it to Olympic athletes who hear an inspirational message: "They may be used to running just one mile, but upon hearing that message, their heart, mind, and body are ready to run five miles, and they achieve it."

**your turn**

Create an iNspiring vision for your life, leadership, or career.

To create inspiring vision, try Gops's approach. Put people first as human beings and individuals. Encourage them to shift how they think about their work. Pinpoint what sustainable, positive impact they want their work to have. Actively engage them in visioning and change. Support them as they strive for greatness.

### Tell Stories

David Craig is an introspective leader and cancer advocate. He serves as co-founder and CEO for GRYT Health, a digital oncology company focused on patient empowerment. A two-time cancer survivor himself, David recognized how telling his story facilitated his healing journey, inspired hope, and created belonging. GRYT's goal is to create collaborative, nonjudgmental, and welcoming space for cancer patients, caregivers, and survivors to share their stories.

When you visit GRYT's site, the first thing you see are beautiful pictures of cancer patients and survivors and their written stories. Prior to her death, Jane Marczewski's story was featured on the main page.[25] Not just a cancer patient, Jane—stage name Nightbirde—was a talented singer and songwriter who performed an original song entitled "It's OK" on *America's Got Talent* in 2021.[26]

Throughout the song, Nightbirde tells the story of her second bout with cancer. She emphasizes that she's more than just the bad experiences she's endured. As she tells Simon Cowell, judge on *America's Got Talent*, the moral of her story is this: "You can't wait until life isn't hard anymore before you decide to be happy."[27]

Nightbirde's storytelling inspired the judges to act. Moved by her story and beautiful voice, Simon gave her the coveted golden buzzer. If you watch her audition (which went viral), have some tissues nearby. David was and is extremely proud of Jane and says, "My greatest hope with GRYT is to inspire people to believe they can do the hard things—even if it's just navigating the initial cancer diagnosis."[28]

To build your storytelling skills, use Nightbirde's approach. Identify your audience. Craft the message you want to share with them. Make the story memorable by including emotion. Use personal examples of overcoming struggles, failures, or barriers to success to make the story relatable. Keep the focus on the audience's benefit. Authentic stories that reveal vulnerability and surmounting challenges inspire others. *They help people hope and believe that anything is possible.*

**your turn**

Craft a personal story that requires you to be vulnerable.

### Lead Authentically

Arabeth Balasko is a professional archivist, historian, and founder of Past is Present, a consulting service specializing in bringing the past into the modern era. Arabeth consults with cultural and public service organizations, helping them create inclusive environments that make stories and histories of diverse voices accessible to all.

While working for AmeriCorps right after college, Arabeth was assigned to a community garden project in West Virginia. She had six months to create a leadership team, find volunteers, and complete the work. If she didn't succeed, the project would lose its grant money. On top of that, Arabeth lacked a green thumb, was in her first people leader role, and struggled to get the project back on track after it had been sitting dormant for years.

Arabeth sought out people willing to serve the local community in various capacities. She was upfront with them about her people leadership inexperience, lack of gardening expertise, and intimidation due to the steep project challenges. But by being vulnerable and letting people know the challenging road ahead, she inspired them to join the journey and achieve greatness together.

In her *Harvard Business Review* article "How to Tell a Great Story," Carolyn O'Hara quotes Nick Morgan, author of *Power Cues*, who reveals why Arabeth's tactic worked: "We actually like to be told that it will be tough going. Smart leaders let people know the road ahead will be difficult. But you won't have to convince them to come along for the ride—they'll join because they want to contribute to something greater than themselves."[29]

Arabeth says the garden project was a great leadership experience for her because she was able to be her authentic self. She explains, "Even if I wasn't quite sure about what I was doing as a people leader, I made sure that the volunteers felt valued as human beings, knew their roles were valued and their contributions acknowledged and appreciated. My leadership style is more collaborative, so this approach felt authentic to me. If I had tried to be someone I'm not, the project wouldn't have succeeded."[30]

Arabeth and her team completed the community garden project on time and within budget. The garden continues today under a different platform, providing the community with fresh produce and jobs for differently abled workers. Due to the garden's success, the community has also attracted additional grants for solar panels and other green solutions.

**your turn**

What is one action you can take to lead more authentically?

To lead authentically, follow Arabeth's advice: "*Anyone can lead authentically; it just takes the willingness to be yourself, lose your ego, be open to newness, and stay human.*"

### Trust First

Early in my career, I worked at Electronic Data Systems (EDS). I was sent on a leadership retreat to Tennessee. For one activity, we had to don climbing equipment, climb to the top of a tall pole, yell "on belay," then jump off the pole. I didn't want to jump because I didn't trust the EDSers (who were strangers) holding the belay ropes to keep me safe.

After much delay and peer pressure, I finally decided to jump. When I got to the ground, one of the guys told me I inspired him, since he "*didn't think women could do things like that.*" Despite the backhanded, sexist comment, I was proud of myself for trusting these people and for inspiring that guy to shift his worldview.

While serving as president and CEO of Starbucks, Howard Behar grew the company from twenty-eight stores to more than fifteen thousand stores on five continents. In his book, Howard describes his approach to trust: "You have to give before you get."[31] In other words, *give trust first to get trust.* If it sounds like reciprocity is involved, you're right. Trusting first reflects a universal law of giving.

Chopra explains that "the law of giving and receiving is based on the fact that everything in the universe operates through dynamic exchange: every relationship is one of give-and-take because giving and receiving are different aspects of the universe's energy flow. If we stop the flow of energy, we interfere with nature's intelligence. We must give and receive in order to keep anything we want circulating in our lives."[32]

In addition to dynamic energy flow, research suggests multiple benefits of trusting first. Rotter conducted studies on interpersonal trust in the 1970s and published his findings in 1980. He found that people who trusted first were "not gullible, were happier overall, were less likely to lie, cheat or steal, respected the rights of others, and were liked more and sought out as a friend more often, by both low-trusting and high-trusting others."[33]

**your turn**

Which beliefs do you need to release to give trust first?

Rotter's findings support those of Zak, whose neuroscience research indicates that trust is a prerequisite for collaboration and teamwork.[34] Trust sparks and ignites our relationships, and trusting first is a key tool in the Human Leader tool kit. *Like the body without oxygen, inspiration can't survive without trust.*

## concluding thoughts

Bob Easton served as a senior managing director at Accenture. His life's purpose is to increase human flourishing every day. Bob says, "I want to inspire others versus intimidate. But I've learned that even a leader's presence can be quite intimidating."[35]

After a recent town hall, a young female analyst who'd been with the firm for six months asked to speak with Bob. When she showed up to his office, she was so scared, she was shaking. She'd written down all of her talking points and told him her story.

She hoped she wouldn't have to leave the firm because she wasn't practicing her skills and was losing confidence in her abilities. She was doing work unrelated to her existing skill set.

When she finished speaking, Bob asked her if she'd told her female leader these things. She said she hadn't, and Bob asked why not. The analyst replied, "She's really intimidating!"

After the analyst left his office, Bob called the analyst's leader. She was surprised to learn her staff perceived her as intimidating. As a leader, *understanding whether your words, actions, behaviors, or presence intimidate or inspire others directly impacts your effectiveness.*

Bob says, "When you're the boss and you say something, it has so much more power." To counteract the intimidation factor, use the tools described in this chapter to evolve your leadership style and inspire others:

- Create a vision to which people can connect
- Tell stories that engage people at the heart level
- Lead authentically and with vulnerability
- Trust first to get trust

Chris Lamb, PhD, is an engaged scholar looking to improve organizational effectiveness who also serves as chief executive officer at Prothya Biosolutions. As a seasoned start-up and technical people leader, he offers his advice: "To be successful, ensure people have needed resources, understand them, and inspire them to perform."[36] Honoring diversity, connecting on a human level, and recognizing each human being's uniqueness inspires higher levels of engagement and performance.

Human Leaders like Chris, Bob, Howard, David, Arabeth, Gops, and Amy understand that creating vision, storytelling, leading authentically, and trusting first are key to being an inspirational leader. Inspiration creates direction and shapes movement of follower actions toward an aspirational future.

## key takeaways

- Inspiration creates direction and shapes movement.
- Inspiring others propels voluntary action.
- Inspiration facilitates agency.
- Inspiration results in getting results.
- Inspiration is important because it creates pictures of possibility.
- Inspiration combined with authenticity begets followership.
- Visionary leaders are more effective than those lacking vision.
- Stories are in our DNA—they're how we learn, love, and live.
- Inauthentic leadership inhibits inspiration.

- Inspiration and distrust cannot coexist.
- Without vision, it's impossible to inspire others.
- Human Leaders engage hearts and inspire action through storytelling.
- Leaders who are their authentic selves inspire others.
- Leaning into, instead of away from, trust expands relationships, human connection, and business results.
- Authentic stories help people believe anything is possible.
- Anyone can lead authentically—just be yourself and stay human.
- Give trust first to get trust.
- Like the body without oxygen, inspiration can't survive without trust.

## 11

# HUMANS framework: seeing

## recognizing the human behind the title

J. Manuel Ocasio (Manny) loves Broadway shows, ardently supports civil and social rights, and is a licensed lawyer pursuing a PhD in strategy and entrepreneurship at the International School of Management in Paris, France. He also happens to serve as chief human resource officer of Luminis Health. Luminis is a community-focused health system with 741 beds and 9,500-plus medical staff, employees, and volunteers.

As chief people officer, Manny is responsible for each soul in every department. During tax season, it's common for the finance and accounting departments to put in long hours. One evening, the payroll manager was working late when an email from the CEO popped into her inbox.

In the email, the CEO asked her to send him W2 forms for every employee—all 2,500 of them. Not about to question the CEO, the manager sent him the requested information. When she came into work the next morning, she asked the CEO if he had received the report.

The CEO said, "What report are you talking about?" The manager instantly felt sick. She realized she had done something egregious. At the same time, the CEO realized the calamitous situation.

The CEO pulled Manny and other people into a meeting. Tensions were high, people were upset, and everyone was look-ing for someone to take the fall. The manager's action had dire consequences: it revealed personal and confidential information about *every* employee in the company.

While quite common now, back in the day, these types of phishing scams around tax time were new, and people didn't know to be wary of them. Manny recalls the top question on everyone's mind: *What would her punishment be for falling for it?* Manny replied: "I believe in *separating the person from the prob-lem.* After careful review of the data, I believe this is an instance of human error. She should not be penalized."[1] Shocked and stunned, the entire room fell silent.

Recognizing the organizational crisis and potential harm to employees due to the W2 data leak, Manny continued: "This is an opportunity for us to act with enormous integrity." He shared a detailed strategy to manage the crisis, communicate to employees, mitigate potential impacts to employees' personally identifiable information, and enhance systems to prevent future issues. Within twenty-four hours of the breach, the company executed the game plan.

They communicated the nature, scope, and timing of the breach. They provided employees with comprehensive, third-party solutions to investigate, protect, and repair their identities. They created systems with checks and balances to prevent future mishaps.

In addition, leadership focused on improving organizational culture. They empowered employees, nurtured collaboration and creativity, and established new cultural norms and expected behaviors. These actions created a high-trust organization, improving communication, interaction, and relationships between management and staff.

Manny reflects on the situation: "In that moment, I led from influence more than authority. *I saw the human in the manager and put her first.* It was a great moment for me as a leader and an opportunity to evolve the organization into a twenty-first century, human-centric health system."

## what does it mean to see others?

In the blockbuster movie *Avatar*, protagonists Jake and Neytiri greet each other by saying *oel ngati kameie*. The verb "kame" in the Na'vi language reflects a singular, almost spiritual meaning: "I see you and recognize you as a whole being."[2]

In the English language, however, the verb "to see" has multiple meanings in this context. One is the physical act of looking at something or someone with the eyes. Another is seeing a person at a deeper, more complex level, recognizing and acknowledging their uniqueness, their humanness.

As Manny's story demonstrates, *viewing someone as more than just an employee enables seeing at a deeper level.* It fosters recognition of the whole human, including strengths and flaws, hopes and dreams, challenges and goals. Viewing the payroll manager as a human being helped Manny humanely lead through the crisis, while allowing the employee to retain her dignity and employment status.

Manny's upbringing, personal challenges, life, and leadership experiences taught him to view employees as people. But most leaders and organizations don't have a human lens, focusing instead on profitability and productivity. Moreover, *they've been professionally trained to engineer humanity out of the workplace.*

This movement started with Frederick Taylor's efforts to enhance industrial efficiency in the early 1900s. Taylor was a mechanical engineer who determined that humans weren't maximizing their work output and tried to make humans produce like machines. Over one hundred years later, dehumanization persists. From the title of the "human resource" department to the language used to reference human beings (headcount, "FTE," asset, resource, and more), evidence of Taylor's handiwork is pervasive.

*Seeing people as human at work counteracts the notion of people as resources.* Seeing others means acknowledging and honoring their humanity. It means recognizing they are human and more than just an employee performing a task or an object to be used and discarded. Seeing others and helping them feel seen are critical skills for creating humane, twenty-first century workplaces.

**your turn**

How do you "see" people at work?

Seeing is the sixth skill in the HUMANS framework.

## why is it important to see others?

*When we don't see others or help others feel seen, it causes separation.* People disengage and we make (often faulty) assumptions about why they've disconnected. Their emotional agility, social interactions, and mental health suffer. Their work quantity or quality declines, they take more "sick" days, and they may even start work later and stop earlier. These reactions may seem a bit over the top, but a quick look at human evolution helps us understand why.

The importance of being seen goes back to prehistoric times. In hunter/gatherer days, not being seen was tantamount to death. If your nomadic tribe members looked around and didn't see you when they were ready to move on to greener pastures, it's likely you would be forgotten and left behind. This meant facing certain death from the elements, other tribes, or big, hungry, faster-than-you carnivorous animals.

Not being seen can cause uncertainty or anxiety. A common example is parents dealing with a tired, stubborn, or spoiled child when out in public. The child refuses to listen to their parents' wishes and sits down in protest. The standoff begins and the parents ultimately resort to threatening the child: "We're leaving now—*with or without you.*"

The parents then walk away. The child seated on the ground watches them walk away, panics, and starts crying. The primitive part of the child's brain senses uncertainty—and even danger—at the potential of being left behind and separated from their parental "tribe."

As Homo sapiens, we're social creatures with innate seeing and belonging needs.[3] Without sufficient social support, our physiological health declines. Research suggests that loneliness results in higher levels of cortisol.[4] Taken to the extreme, separate research studies conducted fifty years apart demonstrate that a lack of social interaction predicted—and unfortunately resulted in—high mortality rates in orphanages.[5]

*Being seen helps people feel they belong, their thoughts and contributions are valued, and their needs are important.* Being seen via social relationships and interaction has positive mental health benefits, decreases mortality, and improves well-being.

When people have strong relationships and interpersonal connections, research points to a 50 percent decrease in mortality risk.[6] Research from Harvard's happiness study supports this and finds that quality relationships are the best predictor of success, well-being, and health throughout our lives.[7]

Leaders must prioritize seeing the human in the worker. Being and feeling seen increases psychological safety, engagement, satisfaction, and motivation levels. Seeing others counteracts the blindness and perils of invisibility.

# what behaviors get in the way of
# helping people feel seen?

Many factors stop us from deeply seeing the human in the beings around us. From the frustration of not being seen ourselves to poor leadership role models rampant in the world today, too often we ignore and overlook the beautiful tapestry of humanity. My research with executives and leaders points to three toxic behaviors: ignoring people, creating division, and dehumanizing others.

### Ignoring People

Kim Wexler is a lawyer in the Netflix series *Better Call Saul*. In one episode, she loses a key, high-value client for her prestigious law firm HHM. As punishment, her boss has her kicked out of her spacious, light-filled, prime real estate office on the top floor. She is relegated to a tiny, dark-paneled basement hovel, devoid of windows and filled with towering stacks of file boxes, and demoted to the special hell of document review.[8]

As Kim's office is no longer near the boss, he literally doesn't see her anymore. Therefore, she's out of sight and no longer top of mind. To her boss, Kim's value as an employee has diminished. But his actions also demonstrate he's no longer interested in her and her potential despite her mistake. *In seeing her as one-dimensional—as just the totality of her work output to the law firm—he devalues her humanity.*

With such diversity, color, and beautiful intricacy of people all around us, it's stunning to consider that "we're not of interest to each other," in poet Elizabeth Alexander's words.[9]

Ignoring someone in the twenty-first century is akin to a pre-historic, nomadic tribe leaving a member behind to face death.

**your turn**

Think of the last time you ignored someone on purpose. What impact did it have?

Purposefully ignoring another person is rude, demeaning, and hurtful.

Every day we have multiple opportunities to see others and help them feel seen. Willfully ignoring people signals your lack of interest in them. Global surveys show that 43 percent of workers feel invisible.[10] This suggests that people in positions of power and influence are perceived as ignoring or not caring about employees, a death knell for leaders.

### Creating Division

José* is a client of mine and is *always* right. Anyone José comes in contact with doesn't have a fighting chance of being seen, since it's all about him and his rightness. Do you know any Josés? Are *you* José?

By behaving in this way, José creates division between him and other people through behavior and binary argument. Since José is always right, by default everyone else is wrong. Binary argument adds up to division.

There's no debate about it—he doesn't consider the other person's point of view or how they see the world. This de facto categorization therefore separates people into two groups: the "right," "correct," or "seen" group and the "wrong," "incorrect," or "invisible" group. But it's not just right and wrong that leads to division and invisibility.

As a child steeped in the tenets of organized religion, I saw division in how people viewed church attendance. There were the weekly, devoted churchgoers (the "us"—my family) versus the "Christmas & Easter" (C&E) people (the "them"—other people). The C&E churchgoers were clearly less devout given they only showed up twice a year.

Accompanied by its evil companions, assumption and judgment, this division created two distinct groups of people. The weekly churchgoers viewed themselves as righteous and pious. On the other hand, the twice-a-year attendees were seen as less serious, lacking devotion, and less worthy of God's love.

As an adult who lived several decades in the environs of Detroit, I often see separation creating invisibility. For example, Eminem sings about how people who live in suburban Detroit view the city. He recounts how their vision suddenly gets blurry when they stand on the north side of 8 Mile Road and look south—8 Mile Road is viewed as the emotional, psychological, and physical ribbon of asphalt separating the city of Detroit from its suburbs. For those who live north of 8 Mile, anything or anyone south of this demarcation line often goes unseen. The Birwood Wall—Detroit's version of the Berlin Wall—still stands along 8 Mile, mirroring a dehumanizing past still reflected in present-day segregation.

Division shifts our perception of people not included in our group—the "outgroup." We view outgroup members as different, potentially less human,[11] and even go as far as to ascribe machine or animal characteristics to them,[12] as the Nazis did to the Jews or the Hutus to the Tutsis.

*Birwood Wall Images copyright Dr. Jennifer Nash, April 16, 2022, Detroit, Michigan, USA.*

Division narrows our field of vision. It biases how we view others. It strips us of our capacity to see others as equal, human, and important.

It is human nature to seek qualities of ourselves in others. We reflect that likeness and commonality in the groups we join, people we befriend, and employees we hire. In doing so, we often perpetuate blindness over seeing, division rather than inclusivity, and homogeneity versus diversity.

**your turn**

How do you create or reduce division between people?

### Dehumanizing Others

Dehumanizing occurs when people are denied their human attributes. There are two types of dehumanization: human uniqueness and human nature. When denied, one form likens people to animals (human uniqueness), while the other likens them to objects or machines (human nature).[13] The table below describes each type's characteristics when attributed or denied.[14]

### types and characteristics of dehumanization

|  | human uniqueness | human nature |
|---|---|---|
| definition | attributes distinguishing humans from other animals | shared and fundamental features of humanity |
| characteristics when attributed | • refinement<br>• civility<br>• morality<br>• higher cognition | • emotionality<br>• warmth<br>• cognitive flexibility |
| characteristics when denied | • explicitly or implicitly likened to animals<br>• viewed as childlike, immature, coarse, irrational, or backward | • explicitly or implicitly likened to objects or machines<br>• viewed as cold, rigid, inert, or lacking emotion |

sources: bastian and leyens, adapted by jennifer nash

Dehumanization examples are all too easy to find. American slave owners bought or sold native Africans as slaves, then assigned them their surnames. German Nazis referenced Jewish people as *untermenschen* (subhumans) and rats, undeserving of moral regard, as Smith notes.[15]

In 1971, Stanford Professor Philip G. Zimbardo launched a study to simulate the psychological effects of imprisonment. Zimbardo's prison experiment had to be stopped after just six days because the "guards" became sadistic and the "prisoners" submissive and depressed.[16] Twenty-four years later, in Rwanda, the Hutus committed atrocious acts of genocide against the Tutsis, whom they called cockroaches.

Fast forward nearly thirty years, research suggests that 39 percent of surveyed Americans blame Asians and Asian Americans for the SARS-CoV-2 coronavirus.[17] Since the start of the 2020 pandemic, Asian hate crimes rose 76 percent while attacks against Black Americans rose 63 percent per the FBI.[18] However, dehumanization isn't just limited to war, genocide, prison simulations, hate crimes, and pandemics.

It's also present at work.

If your boss ignores you, yells at you in front of other people, or forgets your name, that's dehumanization. If you've been excluded from the inner circle, told you're too emotional (usually to women), or too cold and unfeeling (generally to men), you've experienced dehumanization at work.

Remote surveillance also dehumanizes employees. Darrell West says, "Companies are legally allowed to install tracking software on business computers without notifying employees, monitor employee attentiveness through biometric data, track physical movement, and take pictures of employees..."[19]

Surveillance does have its place, but *not* as a way to lead and manage people. Relying on technology to lead and micromanage people and their performance isn't a monitoring issue. It's a power and control issue wrapped in a box devoid of people leadership tools.

In addition, using technology to surveil people's whereabouts and activities during the work day reveals an uglier truth. It treats adults like immature children, dismissing their higher cognition capabilities. Research suggests this denial of human uniqueness (see previous table) negatively impacts employee physical, emotional, and mental health.[20]

Employees who perceive themselves as dehumanized have lower job satisfaction and higher levels of turnover intentions.[21] They are less apt to go above and beyond their normal job duties. They may withdraw or be excluded from social circles at work.

Dehumanizing gets in the way of seeing others and helping others feel seen because it removes humanity from the equation. It negates personhood. It *denies autonomy, demolishes equality, and destroys the human spirit.*

**your turn**

When have you dehumanized another person or experienced dehumanization yourself?

## what tools can you use to get better at helping people feel seen?

We've discussed three barriers that prevent you from seeing others and helping them feel seen. Here are three techniques to get better at seeing others.

## Acknowledgment

Susan David, PhD, is a psychologist at Harvard Medical School and the author of *The Wall Street Journal* bestseller *Emotional Agility*. In her LinkedIn newsletter, Susan shares the story of how the Northern Natal tribes in South Africa acknowledge each other with the Zulu greeting "Sawubona." Translated literally, this greeting means, "I see you, and by seeing you, I bring you into being."[22]

This greeting is deeper than just a perfunctory "how are you?" It speaks to the whole person before you. It validates them as a human being.

Arabeth from Chapter 10 says, "I always strive to stay human. I acknowledge people when I pass them. I think that's important, and it goes a long way."[23]

Acknowledging others recognizes their existence and helps them feel seen. Acknowledging others is a common courtesy and a form of politeness. Acknowledgment combats willful ignorance by recognizing and honoring presence.

## Inclusivity

Pierre Dulaine was born in Jaffa to an Irish Protestant father and a Palestinian Catholic mother. A global citizen fluent in multiple languages, Pierre became a highly accomplished ballroom dancer, winning four World Championship titles with his dancing partner Yvonne Marceau.[24] Upon retiring from competition, Pierre decided to make the world more inclusive through dance.

After founding Dancing Classrooms in New York City in 1984, Pierre returned to Israel with the goal of teaching Jewish and Palestinian children how to dance. In a society with extensive cultural and religious restrictions on interethnic interaction, this seemed a nearly insurmountable task. The cultural divisions were stringent, the emotional tenor highly charged, and the parents' religious beliefs deeply ingrained in their children.

Pierre's journey to create unity and inclusivity in Jaffa is chronicled in the 2013 documentary *Dancing in Jaffa*.[25] In the film, Pierre demonstrates how to invite a partner to dance. He asks, "May I have this dance, please?" and extends his hand, which his partner accepts.

One of the young female students exclaims, "We actually have to *touch* them?" and her young male partner recoils in horror. Pierre says, "My hardest and most important challenge in my life has been to bring Jewish and Palestinian Israeli children together through dance."[26]

In dance, as in life, extending or accepting a hand to hold creates an "us" rather than a "me." It's about unifying two individuals on a shared journey, rather than embarking alone on a solo expedition. *Inclusivity counteracts division by infusing togetherness into the interaction dynamic.*

### See People as Human

On 9/11, one of Manny's colleagues, Judy*, was working at a large downtown DC hospital. As patients from the Pentagon arrived, Judy rushed to triage. One of the incoming patients was grievously injured and severely burnt.

To prevent finger loss due to swelling, Judy cut off the patient's wedding ring. She put it in her pocket for safekeeping.

Judy reassured the man that his wife would get the ring regardless of what happened to him.

Judy's actions demonstrated her care for the whole person: the injured and burned patient as a husband with a loving partner and family affected by this devastating incident. Manny says, "When I learned this, I had an enormous amount of admiration for her as a person, not just as a nurse. It made her human and revealed her vulnerabilities and strengths."[27]

At a different point during his career, Manny was involved in a challenging merger. He had to work with Gerry*, a colleague he didn't see eye to eye with. The relationship was adversarial at best.

Manny and Gerry went on a long road trip together. During their drive, Gerry shared that her mother recently passed away. She confided to Manny that this loss rekindled her desire to deepen her faith, reflected in her passion for and commitment to her work.

Manny previously saw Gerry as a workaholic. However, this information cast her in a completely different light. Being deeply faithful himself, Manny discovered common ground with Gerry. This mutual recognition of each others' humanity improved their working relationship and resulted in a successful merger.

Manny's stereotyping of Gerry as a workaholic reflects the primacy principle. This law is a form of cognitive psychological bias.[28] The common adage "you only get one chance to make a good first impression" stems from this rule. It means that our initial perceptions about someone stick in our minds and can be resistant to change.

Manny's first impression of Gerry was that she worked all the time, hence labeling her a workaholic. From a neuroscience perspective, our brains are wired to take such efficiency short-cuts. However, these biases can be inaccurate and harmful, particularly if not adjusted for evidence to the contrary.

Becoming aware of such biases helps us check our assumptions. Gathering data helps us see others from a multidimensional, whole-person perspective. To see people as human, Manny advises: "Spend time with colleagues to see their different dimensions. Get to know them, their motivations, beliefs, and families. You'll see them in a different, more human light."

Manny expanded his perspective to see Judy outside of her work persona. This action helped him see her as a human being who cared about the patient's emotional health and family too. Manny learned about Gerry's faith, which gave him a completely different perspective on her actions, beliefs, and motivations, adjusted his cognitive bias, and helped him see her as a person.

*Seeing people as human restores their humanity.* It brings to life the positive attributes of human nature and character in vivid technicolor. Seeing people as people first reverses dehumanizing actions, beliefs, and behavior to honor the human in others and help them feel seen.

## what actions can you take to help others feel seen?

The three tools of acknowledgment, inclusivity, and seeing people as human eradicate the respective barriers of ignoring people, creating division, and dehumanizing others. Now let's examine three actions to help you practice these tools.

### Be a Mirror

Actor Omar Sy plays Assane Diop, the protagonist in the Netflix hit series *Lupin*, who consistently outsmarts the police. He is successful not because he is unobtrusive, but because his appearance, mannerisms, language, and behaviors mirror his ever-changing circumstances, adapting like clay in a pottery wheel.

Mirroring is a technique to adopt other people's verbal words and nonverbal expressions, gestures, and energy. With roots in behavioral science, this act of matching others' communication styles builds relational trust.[29] Research has demonstrated inter-human trust building and *human-to-digital assistant* trust building (think Alexa or Siri)![30]

To mirror someone, observe their body language and then imitate it. For example, notice how the person you're speaking with is seated. If they are perched on the edge of the chair, you perch too. If they are leaning back with their hands behind their head, then you do the same. Take note of their arm position—are they crossed or relaxed down at their sides? Observe their seated position and posture, then match it.

Pay attention to the other person's words and repeat the last few words they say. Be cognizant of the energy they exude and meet them at that same vibrational frequency.

◄ ◄ ◄  **pro tip**  ► ► ►

*If you think this whole mirroring thing is too "woo-woo," cheesy, or has negative intent, think again. Mirroring is the FBI's #1 strategy for negotiating.[31]*

► ► ►  ▣  ◄ ◄ ◄

For example, if the other person is highly animated and speaks loudly and quickly, dial up your hand movements, volume, and energy to match. Conversely, if they are calm and speak slowly and quietly, slow your rate of speech and lower your volume to meet them where they are.

Being a mirror means reflecting back to the other person what you observe: what you hear them say; how they think, act, and behave; and how they present themselves to the world. In contrast to ignoring someone, mirroring requires presence and attention to someone else. This effort helps you notice and observe their communication behaviors. It results in others feeling acknowledged and seen, essential to our sense of self and desire to belong.

**your turn**

Mirror one gesture from the other party in your next conversation. What happens?

### Be Inclusive

Alex Toussaint is an intense, wildly popular, and highly motivational Peloton instructor. Early in life, Alex struggled to stay in school and was in and out of trouble. To correct the behavior, Alex's father sent him to military school to instill discipline and structure.

After Alex became a spin instructor at Peloton, his father called him to tell him how proud he was of him. Alex's reaction? He broke down in tears. "I'd waited my entire life for my father to tell me he was proud of me."[32] Alex finally felt seen and validated. Today, Alex credits his military education for saving his life, shaping his mindset, and helping him succeed at his goals.

During spin classes, Alex draws on his military training to shape his approach. His motto is "No rider left behind." This inclusive mindset creates one group or "Peloton" of riders.[33] During spin class, riders virtually high five each other to show solidarity and leave no one behind.

With 2.77 million connected subscribers as of early 2022,[34] Peloton features inclusion as a tenet of its community. Riders join groups such as "Together We Go Far," "Team Activate," or "PelotonNewbies" and add these hashtags to their profiles. Live classes are offered in multiple languages at multiple times.

Joining the Peloton community requires no special work-out equipment, only an app membership. To demonstrate their commitment to inclusiveness, Peloton decreased their signature bike's price, and offered monthly financing with 0 percent interest to reduce entry barriers. With annual revenue exceeding $4 billion in 2021, Peloton has figured out that an inclusive culture attracts new users, engages existing subscribers, decreases subscription churn, and strengthens brand loyalty.[35]

Organizations with inclusive cultures are eight times more likely to realize better business outcomes than those without, per Juliet Bourke.[36] In addition, Dr. Bourke, who was a partner with Deloitte Australia, suggests that employees who feel included have 17 percent higher performance, 20 percent improved decision-making, and 29 percent increased collaboration.[37] These significant outcomes reflect the extent to which seeing others through inclusionary efforts matters.

To be inclusive, ensure that all are seen, welcomed, and valued for their contributions. Create opportunities for connection by bringing people together around a common goal.[38] Empower people to grow and develop as human beings, not just workers. Help people feel they belong and have value as individuals. Treat everyone with respect and ensure they feel safe to voice their opinions.

Gena Cox, PhD, author of the book *Leading Inclusion*, says that "inclusion requires curiosity, connection, and comfort. To be inclusive, demonstrate curiosity, for example, by asking a new person you meet to share an experience or explain how they do something. To build connection and comfort, strike up conversations with people who seem 'different' and spend time in their world." Gena continues: "Inclusion is helping each human you meet feel seen."[39] Helping people feel seen through inclusion isn't just a nice-to-have. It's a must-have, impacting talent attraction and retention, top- and bottom-line results, and organizational longevity.

**your turn**

Identify one action you will take to be more inclusive.

## Be Human

With the Great Reshuffle still foxtrotting its way across the global employment ballroom, the number of job applicants is higher than ever before. For technology jobs in particular, the competition is fierce. How can applicants differentiate themselves from the crowd?

Be human. Ashwin Krishnan created Stand Out in Ninety Seconds, a branding service dedicated to helping tech professionals reveal the human underneath the technical cloak.[40] Ashwin humanizes tech candidates, leaders, and existing employees through video interviews posted on the candidates' social media accounts.

Empathy is a common thread throughout the videos. Empathy helps you see others' needs and become aware of their thinking, emotions, and behaviors. It's in high demand as employers seek emotionally intelligent talent for their organizations. This is because "empathy is a key characteristic of effective leaders," according to Dr. Richard Boyatzis.[41]

◄ ◄ ◄    **pro tip**    ► ► ►

*Being empathetic also helps others see you as higher performing, per the Center for Creative Leadership's research.*[42]

► ► ►    ◄ ◄ ◄

Graham Binks is the CEO of primeFusion Inc. and author of *Trusting Technology*. As a seasoned technical leader, Graham says, "Empathy is at the top of the list for me. I use it every day as a leader to help people feel seen and respected."[43] Graham isn't the only leader who understands the importance of being empathetic and showing his human side.

Remember Gops from Chapter 10? Gops had a client meeting on a hot, sunny day. The client came running in late, looking frazzled. Gops learned the client had walked to the meeting in the hot sun after his taxi broke down, and he wasn't able to hail another one. He offered the client a glass of water and invited him to take a moment to refresh, recenter, and relax. Gops acknowledged his client's human element using empathy. He attended to his client's hydration needs, which helped the client feel seen.

Being human means acknowledging human needs and attending to them, whether it's hydration, nutrition, exercise, screen breaks, or rest. It means showing grace and compassion when you're stressed out, and everyone around you is too. It means showing frustration, sadness, or irritation and that it's okay to not be okay.

Leaders must see people as human beings to help them feel seen. Leaders must lead humanely to infuse the human element into the workplace. Leaders need to acknowledge they're neither heroes nor perfect, so followers can see them as human.

To be human, be yourself. Reconnect with your human element. Accept the whole you—strengths, imperfections, struggles, and all. The art of being human is simple, but not easy. It requires courage to be vulnerable and to reveal and share your true self with the world. *Leaders must be human so that everyone else can be human too.*

**your turn**

Which two actions will you take to be more human at work?

## concluding thoughts

Dr. Marshall Goldsmith has been ranked as the World's #1 Executive Coach, was twice named as the World's #1 Leadership Thinker by Thinkers50, and is a *New York Times* bestselling author. One of Marshall's heroes is Frances Hesselbein, former CEO of the Girl Scouts and winner of the Presidential Medal of Freedom.

When Frances invited Marshall to do a leadership program for the Girl Scouts, he was eager to participate. When he arrived in town, Marshall had been traveling for days and needed to get his laundry done. He asked Frances if they had a facility to do laundry. She told him yes and instructed him to leave his dirty clothes in a pile on his hotel room floor. The next morning, Marshall had breakfast with several Girl Scout leaders. He happened to look up and saw Frances carrying his dirty laundry to the laundry room.

Marshall explains, "Through this small action, Frances sent a large message. Even though she was CEO, she didn't act better than anyone else. She saw herself as a human being just like the staff and volunteers."[44]

When you're a leader, it can be tough to remember you're simply human, like Frances. There's a lot of pressure. It may feel like you're expected to be perfect all the time, have all the answers, and take immediate action. But this isn't a surefire path to success.

Remember Bob Easton from Chapter 10? Bob notes he's most effective when he takes time to slow down and observe what's happening around him. He says, "It's really difficult to lead with heart, unless you make time to notice what's happening, reflect, and contemplate. I'm least effective when I've got myself so busy and tired that I don't see what's happening all around me."[45]

Like Bob has learned, shifting your focus helps you see others so they feel seen. Take artists for example. They are taught to see shapes, colors, and forms, rather than objects, to perceive scenes.[46] Likewise, leaders can be taught to see the kaleidoscopic elements of people rather than a single employee dimension.

Like Bob, Ingrid from Chapter 6 has gained insight through an external focus. What has she learned? Ingrid says, "People want the same thing; everybody just wants to be seen for who they are."[47]

To help others feel seen, see them as multidimensional human beings rather than reducing them to just their role or title at work. Acknowledge the colorful tapestry of their humanity. Show interest in their lives, families, challenges, and dreams. *Recognizing and honoring each person's humanity helps them feel seen.* Changing how we see others changes the quality of our relationships and how we see the world.

## key takeaways

- See people as human rather than objects or resources.
- Being seen helps people feel a sense of belonging.
- Seeing people as one-dimensional devalues their humanity.
- Dehumanizing denies autonomy, demolishes equality, and destroys belonging.
- Seeing people as human restores their humanity.
- Leaders must be human so that everyone else can be human too.
- Recognizing people's humanity helps them feel seen.

# 12

# from hero to human

## leading effectively in
## the twenty-first century

*Sometimes It Pays to Disagree with the CEO*

**m**eet Damian.

Damian Zikakis is a lifelong learner, craft beer lover, caring coach, and the founder of DGZ Coaching. Prior to becoming a coach, Damian served as the director of the Career Development Office at the Ross School of Business at the University of Michigan. With a background in finance, he started his career as an audit manager at Price Waterhouse, eventually rising to become CFO at Coach U and several other global organizations.

One of these global, foreign-owned organizations brought Damian in as CFO for its US subsidiary. As CFO, Damian was responsible for the finance and accounting departments. He set about getting up to speed on his people and processes, opportunities and problems.

Damian soon discovered he had a major issue, as the books were an utter disaster. He identified unreconciled bank accounts. He found books that hadn't been closed appropriately for months.

Damian brought these issues to the controller's attention. After hearing the controller's perspective, Damian understood he simply didn't have the requisite skills to do the job. The controller was fired, and the next day, Damian initiated a search for a new one.

Damian interviewed multiple candidates for the position. For him, fit from technical, behavioral, and cultural perspectives was critical. Knowing it would take a heavy lift to get things in order, Damian wanted candidates to be aware of this right away.

He carefully explained the significant upfront time requirement to each candidate, but added they could expect normal work-life balance once things were in order. One of the stronger candidates was a good fit with Damian's personality and the organizational culture.

She shared with Damian that she was very interested in the role and willing to put in the extra effort to get things cleaned up. She disclosed that she was a single mom with several children and had an ask of him. Was Damian willing to be flexible with how the work was done and allow her to work remotely after hours?

Damian thoughtfully considered their conversation, her prior performance, skillset, and situation. He understood the motivation behind her request. He approached his boss (the CEO) to get his thoughts.

The CEO was inflexible, old-school, and didn't agree with allowing remote work. He believed Damian should hire a different person. Since the last controller "worked hard" until midnight every night at the office, the boss thought the new one should too.

What the CEO didn't see was that the previous controller was spending part of his work day walking around the office and talking with people from 12:00 p.m. to 5:00 p.m. He didn't start working until 5:00 p.m. when everyone else had left. Damian knew the CEO's argument was based on flawed data and multiple assumptions.

Damian also knew that much of the work could be done remotely as it didn't require server access. Although he didn't have support from above, he had support from his peer group—critical, since they were also stakeholders. Despite his boss's misgivings, he hired the candidate, agreeing upfront to the remote work arrangement.

Damian and his new controller came up with a plan that allowed her to get work done at home after her kids were settled. The controller was excited about the opportunity and devoted to her work. She was highly engaged, loyal, efficient, and produced quality work.

The outcome? She cleaned up the books and delivered them well in advance of the deadline. As a result, stakeholders had accurate forecasting data, the business units exceeded their quarterly targets, and the organization reported quarterly earnings on time, driving up the stock price.

Damian says, "This entire experience was meaningful for me because it made such a difference in her and her children's lives.

Trusting her first and allowing remote work showed the CEO that being flexible can work."[1] He continues: "It was an eye-opening experience for the whole organization to embrace flexibility and creativity in solving a problem."

And what happened to that inflexible CEO? He was let go soon thereafter by the parent company due to his actions, behaviors, and beliefs. After seeing the results Damian produced, the parent company wanted a CEO with a more flexible leadership style.

Damian's willingness to grant his controller trust first set the stage for the possibility of remote work. His *capacity for flexibility created an environment welcoming of diversity and inclusion*. His ability to view his controller as a mother and human being created an organizational culture focused on elevating the human element.

Damian's story reflects Human Leadership at its best. He used the HUMANS framework to establish connection, drive understanding, inspire engagement, and build high-trust working relationships. Damian knows that *to be a Human Leader, you have to lead from the heart.*

## bringing it all together

Throughout the book, you've read inspiring stories from diverse executives, people leaders, and other professionals with varied experiences, identities, and ethnicities. You've observed how they applied Human Leader principles and the HUMANS framework to their leadership. You've noted the individual and organizational quantitative *and* qualitative benefits of being a Human Leader and leveraging the HUMANS framework.

As a successful leader, you're always seeking growth, which is why you picked up this book. You like continuous learning, taking action, leading people, and getting results. Now it's time to unleash the power of your Human Leadership potential.

## designing your human leader action plan

Your Human Leader Action Plan (HLAP) offers personalized direction to design your Human Leader journey. It provides a strategic roadmap to put the principles and practices of Human Leadership into action. It clarifies specific steps for you to become the leader you aspire to be.

**your turn**

Design your
Human Leader
Action Plan.

Let's get started!

▷ **Step 1: Complete the HLI (if you haven't already) and have your score report handy.** ..................................................................

Note your overall score: ............ of 335
Note your relationships score: ............ of 45 = ............ %
Note each dimension's score:

- Hearing          ............ of 35 = ............ %
- Understanding    ............ of 45 = ............ %
- Mattering         ............ of 40 = ............ %
- Appreciating     ............ of 50 = ............ %
- Inspiring          ............ of 50 = ............ %
- Seeing            ............ of 70 = ............ %

▷ **Step 2: Assess Results** ...........................................................

What stands out to you about your score?

Where does your overall score fall in relation to what you expected?

Which dimension contains your highest percentage score?

- What factors contribute to this?

Which dimension reflects your lowest percentage score?

- What do you think is driving this?

How do you feel about your scores overall?

*you have the second report, compare and contrast the*
*data. Engage your stakeholder in dialogue. What do each*
*of you observe? Where is there alignment? Where are there*
*differences? What do you think is causing the disconnect?*
*What do you want to do with that information? What does*
*the stakeholder suggest you do to bridge the gap?*

► ► ► ▦ ◄ ◄ ◄

**Step 3: Identify a SMART Goal** ...................................................................

From the lowest scoring dimension, select *one* focus area or goal.
Write it down here: .............................................

If you are struggling to select just one area or you have two
dimensions with equally low scores, consider the following
questions for each possible goal:

- What would it feel like to be seen as someone who achieves
  this goal?


- What will happen if I don't realize this desired outcome?


- How is this goal meaningful to me?

- How would my life and the lives of those around me be different if I significantly improve in this area?

- Which area would have the greatest impact on my success?

After answering the questions and considering your responses, which focus area do you choose? ...............................................

Make your goal concise and SMART (specific, measurable, achievable, relevant, and timely). Reference examples of SMART goals for guidance.[2]

Write your concise SMART goal here.

◄ ◄ ◄ **pro tip** ▶ ▶ ▶
*Ensure your goal statement includes a specific date for completion as well as observable outcomes to validate your progress. Deadlines create focus and prompt prioritization. Measurable goals facilitate progress evaluation.*
▶ ▶ ▶ ▦ ◄ ◄ ◄

▷ **Step 4: Take Inventory**

Resources

- What resources do you *currently have* that will help you move toward your goal? List them here.



- What resources do you *need* to help you succeed? List them here. *Select examples include: new people leader tools, special projects or stretch assignments, operating processes, awareness of mental models, new beliefs, positive behaviors, new employer, dedicated time, or upskilling*



People

- Who is on your team or personal board of directors to provide support? *This could include an executive, leadership, or behavioral coach; peers; colleagues; friends; family; therapist; teachers; religious figures; or others*
- What type of support does each person contribute? *Examples include: moral, mental, or emotional support; expertise, advice, or guidance; self-care championing; accountability; kick-in-the-ass motivation; or others*

Person: ................................. Support Type: .................................

Person: ................................. Support Type: .................................

Person: ...............................    Support Type: ...................................

Person: ...............................    Support Type: ...................................

Person: ...............................    Support Type: ...................................

Person: ...............................    Support Type: ...................................

Risk

- What barriers might get in the way of your reaching your goal? List them here.

- For each barrier, how will you mitigate the risk of failure? List the contingency plan for each barrier here.

- What are the other concerns, worries, or unknowns regarding this journey?

- What will you do to overcome these challenges?

▷ **Step 5: Execute Your Plan**

Based on your answers above, consolidate your action plan here:

- What is your goal?

- How are you going to execute this goal?

- By when will you achieve this goal?

- Where will you do this?

- Who will provide you support if needed?

- How will you measure your success?

- How will you know you've achieved your goal?

*Track your progress as you work toward your goal. Use the Human Leader Action Plan (HLAP) tracking form available at my website if desired. Alternatively, try a task tracking tool of your choice, such as TickTick, Any. do, Google Tasks, Asana, Microsoft 365, or Trello. Google "daily task tracking apps" for other ideas.*

► ► ►  ▓  ◄ ◄ ◄

If you couldn't wait to jump in and already took action on your plan, then you might be ready to take it to the next level. Evaluate your progress and iterate as needed. Use Steps 6 and 7 below for guidance.

## ▷ Step 6: Evaluate and Iterate

- Use the tracking form to review your completed actions on a weekly or monthly basis.

- If you're not satisfied with your progress, have been interrupted or fallen off track, iterate as needed to help you progress and get back on the path toward your goal.

- At your target completion date, evaluate your progress. Did you meet your goal? ........ If so, move to Step 7.

- If you didn't meet your goal by your deadline, be honest with yourself. What happened? What did you allow to get in the way of your success? List these factors here:

- What will you do differently to succeed in the next go-round? Do you need to engage a coach or accountability partner for support? Update your plan with these actions.

- Continue to evaluate and iterate until you meet your goal.

◄ ◄ ◄ **pro tip** ► ► ►

*If you didn't meet your goal, refer back to the HUMANS framework outlined in Chapter 5 related to your goal. Review each behavioral barrier. Which (if any) of these got*

*in your way? Were there any other barriers that popped*
*up? Study each tool. Is there a technique that might*
*have been helpful? Is there a skill you need to acquire?*
*Consider the actions. How might you integrate any of*
*these into your action plan to help you progress?*

► ► ► ▦ ◄ ◄ ◄

► **Step 7: Celebrate**

You completed your plan and accomplished your goal—well done
and congratulations!

- How will you celebrate this important accomplishment? List
  this here.

- With whom, where, and by when will you celebrate? List this
  here:

- How, to whom, and by when will you show gratitude? List this
  here:

◄ ◄ ◄   **pro tip**   ► ► ►

*Pull out your HLI results. Select another HUMANS dimension you'd like to strengthen. Repeat Steps 1–7 in this chapter to create and execute a new action plan.*

► ► ►   ▦   ◄ ◄ ◄

To level up even more, review each behavior, tool, and action discussed throughout the book. Make a list of ineffective behaviors and limiting beliefs you want to change, helpful tools you want to learn, and specific actions you want to practice. Create an action plan for each one and make this part of your annual goal setting or professional development efforts. Specify how you will continue to build and practice these skills going forward.

## one step closer

Congratulations—you've created your custom Human Leader Action Plan. Well done! You now have everything at your fingertips to start executing your plan. You're one step closer to becoming the Human Leader you aspire to be.

As we saw throughout the book, the days of the "CEO as commander" are dead. Leadership is no longer a solitary, know-it-all, or command-and-control activity. Reclaiming and honoring your humanity and helping others do the same is the new normal in the twenty-first century. Becoming a Human Leader will dramatically and positively impact your life, leadership, relationships, and career and those of your stakeholders as well.

## key takeaways

- Flexibility creates diverse and inclusive environments.
- Human Leaders lead from the heart.
- Deadlines create focus and prioritize effort.
- Measurable goals facilitate progress evaluation.
- You're not alone on the journey.
- It's okay to ask for help.
- Human Leaders include and engage all stakeholders.
- Tracking goal progress feels good and reinforces learning.
- Human Leaders honor and celebrate humanity.

conclusion

# from chaos to doubled revenues in seven months

Let's dive deeper into what made Olivia from Chapter 4 so successful.

Dr. Olivia Croom, DDS, founded Dancing Zebras, a social entrepreneurial organization offering sugar-free drinks to promote childrens' oral health. Prior to her entrepreneurial venture, she served as CDO (chief dental officer) for multiple dental organizations.

As CDO, Olivia built a solid reputation for turning around failing dental clinics. She decided to interview for a leadership role at a poorly run center in Indianapolis. Prior to the interview, she arranged for an office visit to talk with staff and patients and assess the landscape.

On the day of the interview, she met with the company's president. Based on what she learned during her office visit, she told the president she would turn around the failing office in six months and committed to doubling revenues. His response?

He laughed at her.

Yet he still hired her since he trusted her, knew she understood the lay of the land, and liked her chutzpah. He told the clinic's lead doctor, *"You've got a live one here."*

When she arrived at the clinic for her first day on the job, it was utter chaos. In Olivia's words, "It was as if the natives were running the place."[1] They had highly skilled staff, hygienists, and dentists, but no one was leading.

Olivia notes: "The lead doctor was an excellent clinician, but he did not like leading people." There were some standard operating processes and procedures, but they weren't being followed. It was a beautiful office with ugly problems.

Based on her own experience building a successful practice from the ground up, Olivia knew the importance of strong leadership. She utilized all of the learning from her practice management and leadership classes to transform the failing clinic. She built relationships, rolled up her sleeves, and set clear expectations.

Olivia says, "When you listen and participate rather than dictate, people are more willing to trust you." The staff, hygienists, and clinicians saw Olivia's willingness to listen and participate in every area. In turn, they worked hard to meet her high expectations.

Olivia established a weekly status report and delivered it to the president. She updated him on her activities and accomplishments and provided awareness of roadblocks. This operational transparency further expanded their high-trust relationship and set the tone for the clinic's new standard operating processes.

Olivia accomplished the turnaround in seven months, rather than six. Although her estimate was slightly off, Olivia made up for it by *more than doubling revenues*. Her office went from the worst-performing to the best-performing office in the company.

How did she do it?

Olivia set guidelines regarding wait times. She told the staff, "I don't want anyone's butt in a waiting room seat more than fifteen minutes. Ideally, as soon as they sit down, I want them to pop back up like popcorn because you're calling them in." Especially in pediatric dental clinics, short wait times are critical to successful patient treatment.

She made the office a fun environment the staff would enjoy coming to. She rewarded the staff well for their efforts. Olivia bought small gifts to show her staff appreciation for their hard work and treated them to monthly dinners.

Olivia's story illustrates how executing the principles and practices of Human Leadership leads to outstanding results. Her ability to trust first shifted organizational culture. Her focus on recognizing and thanking staff for their efforts helped them feel appreciated. Listening to staff and patients' concerns and challenges helped them feel heard and understood. The tools of the HUMANS framework provided her a roadmap to turn around the clinic's performance through people.

## looking back

Whew—this book has covered a lot of ground! Let's take a quick look back to see where we've been. As you read this brief overview, make a mental note of chapters or specific topics you'd like to go back and review.

John's* story in Chapter 1 revealed multiple pain points due to his people leadership techniques. You noticed how his actions, behaviors, and beliefs hindered him from leading others effectively. His style kept him stuck in the past despite challenges requiring a more dynamic approach.

In contrast, Alan's story in Chapter 2 demonstrated the extent to which twenty-first century leadership facilitates growth for all stakeholders. Alan created a high-trust environment inspiring everyone to elevate their performance and realize their best self. You observed how Alan's actions, behaviors, and beliefs are founded in human and relational leadership skills, which form the future of leadership—Human Leadership—and the future leader—the Human Leader.

In Chapter 3, Markeshia* illustrated the perils of turning off your internal GPS and losing personal connection. You learned why it's critical to lead yourself first and that Human Leadership starts with honoring the human you. You exercised your reflection muscle to complete the Five Steps to Leading Yourself First and begin your journey to Human Leadership.

You met Geneva in Chapter 4, whose fluency in building and nurturing relationships was a master class in honoring others' humanity. You saw from Ellen, Hugh, Alan, Tarina, and Karl that *every* interaction is an opportunity to start, stop, or sustain a relationship. You gained awareness of how leading others requires human-to-human connection, that giving positive value to others increases connection, and that relationships form the foundation of the HUMANS framework.

Chapter 5 introduced the research-based HUMANS framework with its six dimensions of Hearing, Understanding, Mattering, Appreciating, iNspiring, and Seeing. You evaluated your Human Leader capabilities through the Human Leadership Index and interpreted your results. You acquired newfound insight into how the art of Human Leadership is a masterpiece requiring practice, skill, and patience.

Ingrid illustrated how business results, leadership success, and organizational culture depend on hearing others and helping them feel heard in Chapter 6. You learned that hearing others helps people feel respected, valued, and validated. Asking questions, gathering facts, and paraphrasing are tools to gain awareness of peoples' needs, perspectives, and experiences and help them feel heard.

Allie shared how prioritizing understanding stakeholders delivered a successful human resource transformation project in Chapter 7. Ann, Shira, Allie, and Gops demonstrated that listening, perspective taking, and empathy are effective Human Leader tools to understand others. You learned how understanding who people are, what's important to them, and what they prioritize helps people feel understood and is part of the magic of Human Leadership.

In Chapter 8, Tricia dazzled Detroit's bridal industry by helping distressed brides feel they mattered. Suspending judgment and prioritizing people are two actions that help people feel valued. You added the MATTER model to your operating model and realized that as a Human Leader, one of the most important things you can do is show people how much you value them.

Marilyn's story in Chapter 9 exemplifies how her "Wall of Appreciation" helped her teachers and staff feel appreciated for all of their hard work and sacrifice during extraordinary times. You saw from Ken*, Shira, Brad, Damian, and Tracy how demonstrating appreciation is a powerful leadership strategy that also appreciates the bottom line. To help others feel appreciated, you added expressing gratitude to your Human Leader tool kit.

Chapter 10 invited you into the military world, where Brad's commander transformed 3,500 hearts and minds within ninety days through an inspiring vision. You contributed crafting vision, storytelling, leading authentically, and trusting first maneuvers to your Human Leader toolbox. You progressed your HUMANS framework knowledge via the iNspiration dimension and expanded your thinking on trusting people first.

As the sixth and final dimension of the HUMANS framework, seeing was introduced in Chapter 11. In a time of crisis, Manny saw his employee as a human being rather than an inanimate resource, which helped her feel seen. Acknowledging others, being inclusive, and seeing people as human are three key tools in the Human Leader's repertoire. You learned that the art of being human is simple but not easy, and that leaders must be human rather than heroes so that everyone else can be human too.

Damian's story of trusting his new controller to work remotely and realizing outstanding results kicked off Chapter 12. You completed your personalized Human Leader Action Plan. You gained foundational knowledge of the HUMANS framework and are now prepared to put the operating principles and practices of Human Leadership into action.

## taking a step forward

Grab your Human Leader Action Plan. It's time to execute. What specifically are you going to do, how and where are you going to do it, and by when? Drop me a note at *www.drjennifernash.com* and let me know!

## final thoughts

The human element of business often seems to be an oxymoron. People comprise organizations. However, leadership and managers often forget that it's those exact souls who are at the heart of organizations.

They forget that without people, there is no one to create or execute strategy. There are no profits, process, or progress. And there is no one to lead.

But even when there are people to lead, we often forget to equip them with proper people leadership tools. We don't teach them how to be people leaders. We just promote them and expect them to figure things out.

While most leaders have positive intentions and want to lead people well, they aren't aware of blind spots impacting their effectiveness. The horror stories about toxic leaders reveal that awareness gap. As a result, people, organizations, and society pay dearly. The pandemic revealed those heavy costs more clearly than ever before.

It also revealed a naked truth: organizations desperately need better, more effective leaders. Leaders who aren't afraid to be perfectly imperfect, vulnerable, courageous, and human. Leaders who lead people humanely. Leaders who make workplaces human by putting people before profits.

This book offers a solution: Human Leadership. This book provides a foundational tool: the HUMANS framework. This book defines a roadmap: your Human Leader Action Plan. I invite you to join the Human Leader team and change the world by elevating your life, leadership, and career.

Discover valuable human leader resources, including an online human leader index, at the QR code below.

www.behumanleadhuman.com
#behumanleadhuman

# curated
# learning resources

These hand-selected resources include several of my all-time favorites and are intended to amplify your *Be Human, Lead Human* experience. I do not receive affiliate commissions for any of these items. If you find this book or one of the curated learning resources below particularly helpful, I'd love to hear about it! Drop me a note at *www.drjennifernash.com*. Peruse, read, watch, practice, explore, create, dance, and play at your leisure. Enjoy!

## chapter 1

### Leadership Actions

- To learn more about Sheldon Yellen's human element perspective and 9,200 handwritten cards per year, read this: *www.businessinsider.com/ceo-writes-7400-employee-birthday-cards-each-year-2017-6*

■ To gain additional insights into how 181 organizations put people first, take a look at the Business Roundtable's 2021 updated statement on corporations' purpose: *purpose. businessroundtable.org*

### Leadership Behaviors & Styles

■ For behavioral styles, theory, and managerial applications of leadership, reference Bass's seminal work: *www.amazon. com/Bass-Handbook-Leadership-Managerial-Applications-ebook/dp/B0013TX7XY*

■ If Bass's 1,500 page–plus tome is too much, then skim Martinuzzi's seven leadership styles in Doyle's article: *www. americanexpress.com/en-us/business/trends-and-insights/articles/ the-7-most-common-leadership-styles-and-how-to-find-your-own*

### Leadership Beliefs & Thinking

■ David Hutchens delivers business learning through fables. Meet Boogie the Caveman's limiting beliefs: *www.amazon. com/Shadows-Neanderthal-Illuminating-Organizations-Learning/dp/0692782303*

■ Read this *Wall Street Journal* article to learn about several companies that prioritize where work is done: *www.wsj. com/articles/return-to-work-the-boss-wants-you-back-in-the-office-11627079616*

### Leadership Training

■ To learn more about the significant time gap between people leader promotion and training, pick up a copy of

Jacob Morgan's book *The Future of Work*: *www.amazon.com/dp/B00JJ42QKA*

## Remote Work (WFH)

- WFH is not new; our hunter-gatherer ancestors were the first to work from home! Learn more: *www.flexjobs.com/blog/post/complete-history-of-working-from-home*
- Status quo of being in the office five days a week is no longer attractive, says McKinsey's research: *www.mckinsey.com/business-functions/people-and-organizational-performance/our-insights/what-employees-are-saying-about-the-future-of-remote-work*
- The pandemic opened Pandora's WFH box. Learn what people are willing to give up to keep WFH: *www.meetbreeze.com/blog/employees-give-up-benefits-salary-remain-remote*

## The Great Resignation, The Tsunami Turnover, or the Great Reshuffle

- Without employers delivering meaningful and purposeful work, people choose to vote with their feet: *www.bbc.com/worklife/article/20210629-the-great-resignation-how-employers-drove-workers-to-quit*
- Microsoft's 2022 Work Trend Index's statistics suggest how employee priorities have shifted, indicating the Great Resignation is far from over: *www.microsoft.com/en-us/worklab/work-trend-index*

# chapter 2

I'm not the first to proclaim the importance of putting people first, leading with heart, and being human at work, and I won't be the last. For additional perspectives on Human Leadership, working together, and prioritizing the human element, here are several of the plethora of authors, speakers, leaders, and leadership thinkers who have inspired me on my book journey.

### Being Human

- Learn which branch of science holds the answers to what makes us human per James Calcagno and Agustín Fuentes in their 2012 article: *onlinelibrary.wiley.com/doi/full/10.1002/evan.21328*
- Sometimes it may feel like we need permission to be human at work, explains MaryBeth Hyland: *www.amazon.com/Permission-Be-Human-Conscious-Values-Driven/dp/1737288818*
- Deloitte's Erica Volini pens her perspective on positioning human versus employee experience: *deloitte.wsj.com/articles/employee-experience-tryhuman-experience-01565830929*

### Human Leadership

- Sesil Pir shares who gets promoted into people leadership and why Human Leadership is in short supply: *www.forbes.com/sites/sesilpir/2018/11/28/human-leadership-what-it-looks-like-and-why-we-need-it-in-the-21st-century*
- To learn how COVID highlighted the importance of addressing well-being, read Mark Livingston's piece:

www.forbes.com/sites/forbestechcouncil/2021/04/30/why-human-leadership-over-business-leadership-is-the-need-of-the-hour

- "Radically human" is how Gary Burnison, CEO of Korn Ferry, views the future of leadership: www.businessinsider.com/korn-ferry-ceo-radically-human-leadership-tips-2021-3

- Gary Hamel shares how to free the human spirit: www.humanocracy.com

- Leading humans requires a healthy relational climate, the dimensions and outcomes of which I explore through Boyatzis's and Rochford's RCS scale in my dissertation: drjennifernash.com

### Leading with Heart

- Gary Burnison, CEO of Korn Ferry, recounts how being radically human involves leading with heart and why bright red cowboy boots matter to him: www.kornferry.com/insights/special-edition/leading-with-heart

- If you've ever wondered about connecting what you love to do with your work, read Hesselbein, Goldsmith, and McArthur's book: www.amazon.com/Work-Love-Made-Visible-Collection/dp/1119513588

- Mark Crowley suggests that leading with heart is the way forward as traditional leadership practices fail: www.amazon.com/Lead-Heart-Transformational-Leadership-Century-dp-1401967604/dp/1401967604/

### Putting People First

- Read *Talent Wins* by co-authors Ram Charan, Dominic Barton, and Dennis Carey to learn *who* must lead the talent imperative: *www.amazon.com/ Talent-Wins-Playbook-Putting-People/dp/1633691187*
- Best Buy's former CEO Hubert Joly shares leadership principles for the future in his book: *www.amazon.com Heart-Business-Leadership-Principles-Capitalism/dp/1647820383*
- Companies who address employee needs realize significant benefits in *Inc.*'s article: *www.inc.com/t-mobile/ benefits-of-a-people-first-culture.html*
- Marriott walks the talk when it comes to putting people first, as Hougaard shares: *www.forbes.com/sites/ rasmushougaard/2019/03/05/the-power-of-putting-people-first*
- For strategies involving putting people first, read Deloitte's Karen Pastakia's advice: *www2.deloitte.com/content/dam/ Deloitte/global/Documents/About-Deloitte/gx-workforce-strategies-that-put-your-people-first.pdf*

### "Working Together" Management System

- Watch Alan Mulally explain his "Working Together" system at the 2016 Willow Creek Global Leadership summit: *vimeo.com/288951968/bb8a730e41*
- While CEO of Ford Motor Company, Alan worked with Marshall Goldsmith as his executive coach. Watch this webinar of Marshall interviewing Alan in December 2020 as they walk through "Working Together": *www.youtube. com/watch?v=QN6IyAM3bGE*

- James Lewis describes the twelve principles of Alan Mulally's "Working Together" system in his book: *www.amazon.com/Working-Together-Principles-Excellence-Organizations/dp/158798279X*
- Bryce Hoffman recounts how Alan Mulally saved Ford Motor Company using the "Working Together" system: *www.amazon.com/American-Icon-Mulally-Fight-Company/dp/0307886069*
- Marli Guzzetta details four strategic elements of Alan Mulally's "Working Together" system: *www.inc.com/marli-guzzetta/how-alan-mulally-turned-ford-around-inc5000.html*

## chapter 3

### Accountability Team

- Read my perspective on how to build an accountability team, another way your personal "Board of Directors" can support you: *drjennifernash.com*

### Flow

- Mihaly Csikszentmihalyi's masterpiece *Flow: The Psychology of Optimal Experience* is a must-read: *www.amazon.com/Flow-Psychology-Experience-Perennial-Classics-dp-0061339202/dp/0061339202*

### Identity & The Self

- If you struggle with I "should" or "ought," Heinzen provides an excellent three selves overview in his article

"The Social Self" found here: *us.sagepub.com/sites/default/files/03_heinzen_the_social_self.pdf*

▧ Understanding how others view your ideal or best self is critical to your life, leadership, and career. Take the Reflected Best Self Exercise from the University of Michigan: *reflectedbestselfexercise.com/about*

### Leading Yourself First

▧ Stedman Graham discusses the criticality of leading yourself first in his book *Identity Leadership*: *www.amazon.com/Identity-Leadership-Others-First-Yourself/dp/1546083375*

▧ If you're questioning the difference between managing and leading, you're not alone. Take a look at Kotter's article to learn the difference: *hbr.org/2013/01/management-is-still-not-leadership*

▧ Kethledge and Erwin discuss the power of solitude and carving out space for quiet reflection to impact clarity, creativity, emotional balance, and moral courage in their book *Lead Yourself First*: *www.amazon.com/Lead-Yourself-First-Inspiring-Leadership/dp/1632866323*

### Reflection & Learning

▧ Not everyone enjoys reflecting, but Jennifer Porter highlights in her *HBR* article why you should, even if you don't like to: *hbr.org/2017/03/why-you-should-make-time-for-self-reflection-even-if-you-hate-doing-it*

▧ Donald Schön describes "reflection-in-action" in *The Reflective Practitioner*, highlighting how professionals solve problems. Fair warning: this one is rather academic! *www.amazon.com/Reflective-Practitioner-Professionals-Think-Action/dp/0465068782*

- John Dewey posits that "reflection is the only 'potent antidote' to resolve erroneous beliefs" in his 1910 classic *How We Think*: *www.amazon.com/How-We-Think-John-Dewey-ebook/dp/B005UFW3CS*
- David Kolb developed "experiential learning," a four-step process involving reflection, which you can explore: *www.amazon.com/Experiential-Learning-Experience-Source-Development/dp/0133892409*

### Strengths & Habits

- You're not the only one overusing your strengths, as Kaplan deftly explains in his *HBR* article with Kaiser. To learn how to find balance, read this: *hbr.org/2009/02/stop-overdoing-your-strengths*
- There are many strengths assessment options, such as CareerLeader, VIA Character Strengths, or CliftonStrengths; links are in Chapter 3's endnotes. I recommend CareerLeader for its primary focus on workplace application. *Note that CareerLeader offers University of Michigan Alumni Association members a discount via the UMAA website.*
- To understand more about how and why understanding your strengths makes you more effective, review Mind Tools' article on strengths-based leadership here: *www.mindtools.com/community/pages/article/strengths-*

*based-leadership.php?route=pages/article/strengths-based-leadership.php*

▦ James Clear's *Atomic Habits* is a crucial read to gaining clarity on effective habits and why they matter: *www.amazon.com/Atomic-Habits-James-Clear/dp/1847941834*

### Values & Why

▦ Download a free thought-starter list of values at my website: *drjennifernash.com*

▦ Watch Simon Sinek's engaging TED Talk with over 58 million views on finding purpose: *www.ted.com/talks/simon_sinek_how_great_leaders_inspire_action*

### "Start with Why"

▦ Read McKinsey's thoughts on purpose, particularly relevant in times of crisis: *www.mckinsey.com/business-functions/organization/our-insights/igniting-individual-purpose-in-times-of-crisis*

▦ For additional thought-starters on your motivators, try these life-changing questions: *programs.clearerthinking.org/lcq.html#.XuVQUkVKio5*

▦ Clayton Christensen's TED Talk on life success is here: *www.youtube.com/watch?v=tvos4nORfY*. And here in *HBR*: *hbr.org/2010/07/how-will-you-measure-your-life*

▦ Read my perspectives on how to identify your personal values in my popular *HBR* article "What Are Your Personal Values?": *https://hbr.org/2020/11/what-are-your-personal-values*

# chapter 4

### Give & Take in Relationships

▪ Listen to and watch Adam Grant discuss givers, takers, and matchers in his TED Talk that's been viewed over three million times: *www.youtube.com/watch?v=YyXRYgjQXXo*

▪ Adam Grant's book *Give and Take: A Revolutionary Approach to Success* is a bestseller: *www.amazon.com/ Give-Take-Helping-Others-Success/dp/0670026557*

▪ If you're on the fence about giving rather than taking, check out Jeff Bradford's advice here: *www.forbes.com/sites/ forbesagencycouncil/2018/07/19/the-reciprocity-principle-giving-to-get/?sh=2d096dfa2175*

▪ Psychologist Robert Cialdini's classic *Influence: The Psychology of Persuasion* is a must-read: *www.amazon.com/ Influence-Psychology-Persuasion-New-Expanded/dp/ 0063138808*

### Human Connection

▪ For tips on creating connection in the workplace, read Brodkin and Pallathra's *HBR* article: *hbr.org/2021/10/ getting-back-to-the-basics-of-human-connection*

▪ To learn from a biological and neuroscientific perspective why we are wired to connect with each other, take a look at Gareth Cook's excellent *Scientific American* article: *www. scientificamerican.com/article/why-we-are-wired-to-connect*

▪ Charles Ashworth explores separating factors despite technological connection in his *Forbes* article: *www.*

*forbes.com/sites/forbeshumanresourcescouncil/2019/08/01/*
*are-we-losing-the-human-connection/?sh=258ebbd35baa*

### Humble Leadership

- Check out the Scheins' book, *Humble Leadership:
  The Power of Relationships, Openness, and Trust*:
  *www.penguinrandomhouse.com/books/567575/
  humble-leadership-by-edgar-h-schein-and-peter-a-schein*

### Operating Model & Relationships

- When you deploy a relational operating model,
  relationship building is built into the model as its name
  suggests. It doesn't require you to carve out extra time
  on your calendar to build relationships. It doesn't require
  that you spend hours singing "Kumbaya" together. And
  in a fast-paced environment, it doesn't rely on a time-
  inefficient process of "earning" trust—each person gives
  trust freely. Trust is a foundational part of the operating
  process. Reference Chapter 2's "Working Together"
  Management System curated learning resources for tips
  on how to build your relational operating model.

### Trust

- Dr. Dennis Reina and Dr. Michelle Reina are trust
  researchers. Read *Trust and Betrayal in the Workplace* for
  their belief on why trust should be earned *first* rather than
  given: *www.amazon.com/Trust-Betrayal-Workplace-Relationships-
  Organization/dp/1626562571*

- In contrast to Dr. Reina and Reina's work, Stephen Covey presents his case for why trusting faster improves outcomes and decreases cost in his classic bestseller *The Speed of Trust*: *www.amazon.com/SPEED-Trust-Thing-Changes-Everything/dp/074329730X*
- I'd be remiss to not mention Brené Brown's excellent work on the anatomy of trust here.
    - Watch her SuperSoul Sessions talk: *brenebrown.com/videos/anatomy-trust-video*
    - Take the BRAVING inventory: *brenebrown.com/resources/the-braving-inventory*
    - Read *Braving the Wilderness*: *brenebrown.com/book/braving-the-wilderness*
- Roderick Kramer presents an interesting viewpoint of tempered trust in this *HBR* article: *hbr.org/2009/06/rethinking-trust*
- The Workforce Institute released findings on workplace trust—perhaps shedding light on why it still seems to be lacking: *workforceinstitute.org/wp-content/uploads/2020/12/Trust-in-the-Modern-Workplace-Final.pdf*

### Time

- Time is one of the scarcest resources we have. Learn how CEOs manage it in this fascinating piece from Porter and Nohria. Then ask yourself, *How do I stack up?*: *hbr.org/2018/07/how-ceos-manage-time*
- Track 168 hours out of your life to learn how you are really spending your time with Laura Vanderkam's free

tool available: *lauravanderkam.com/manage-your-time*. Read her book to learn how to maximize your time based on your results: *www.amazon.com/168-Hours-Have-More-Think/ dp/1591843316*

## chapter 5

### Dance & Leadership

- Patrice Tanaka shares how her ballroom dance journey made her a more effective CEO in *Becoming Ginger Rogers*: *www.amazon.com/dp/B005FYF4JS*
- Megan Morrison highlights benefits of dance for leaders, even if they think they have two left feet: *trainingmag.com/ how-to-dance-your-way-to-better-leadership*
- Visit my website to learn more about in-person, dance-based leadership development workshops: *www. drjennifernash.com*
- Read my thoughts on how dance makes me a better CEO and entrepreneur here: *www.linkedin.com/pulse/ flow-dancing-becoming-better-leader-jennifer-nash-phd- mba-bcc*

### Relationships

- Read my friend and REx colleague Darin Rowell's perspectives on traits of work relationships: *hbr.org/2019/ 08/3-traits-of-a-strong-professional-relationship*
- Mind Tools has an excellent overview of how to build workplace relationships. Read their suggestions here: *www.*

*mindtools.com/community/pages/article/good-relationships.php?route=pages/article/good-relationships.php*

- Leaders and coaches who focus on relational quality improve outcomes as my and others' research shows. Read Stephens, Heaphy, and Dutton's work to learn how to build high-quality relational connections: *www.researchgate.net/publication/259780637_High-quality_Connections*

# chapter 6

## Auditory Physiology

- If you're into science and biology, you'll love these National Institute of Health hearing physiology items: *www.nidcd.nih.gov/health/how-do-we-hear* and *www.nidcd.nih.gov/health/journey-of-sound-video*
- Listen to or read NPR's article with sound effects on how hearing shapes the evolution of our brains: *www.npr.org/sections/health-shots/2015/09/10/436342537/how-sound-shaped-the-evolution-of-your-brain*

## Communication & Listening

- Ready for more graduate-level hearing work? Take a look at Ximena Vengoechea's excellent book *Listen Like You Mean It*: *www.amazon.com/Listen-Like-You-Mean-Reclaiming/dp/B08D6ZP4F1*
- Interrupting is often viewed as rude. But if it's for the purpose of helping others get their voices heard, is it rude,

or is it inclusive? *hbr.org/2021/03/how-interruptions-can-make-meetings-more-inclusive*

### Culture & Change

▤ Harvard Business School professor John Kotter explains why culture eats strategy for breakfast in *The Heart of Change*: *www.amazon.com/The-Heart-of-Change-audiobook/dp/B001308X6A*

▤ Digital transformation is a hot topic, yet the human element is often forgotten, putting change efforts in peril. Read Tabrizi's point of view: *hbr.org/2019/03/digital-transformation-is-not-about-technology*

### Fact-Checking

▤ In addition to Dr. Gray's tips in Chapter 6's endnotes, review PolitiFact's seven-step fact-check framework here: *www.politifact.com/article/2014/aug/20/7-steps-better-fact-checking*

### Psychology

▤ To learn more about interpersonal behavior, read Argyle's classic *The Psychology of Interpersonal Behavior*: *www.amazon.com/Psychology-Interpersonal-Behaviour-Penguin-ebook/dp/B002RI9VH6*

▤ We are all biased. And these biases impact our beliefs. For an excellent overview of how human bias impacts fact-checking, reference this 2020 *Scientific American* article by Ceci and Williams: *www.scientificamerican.com/article/the-psychology-of-fact-checking1*

## Questions & Socratic Method

▧ As children, asking questions is second nature, yet it's beaten out of us by the time we reach adulthood. Read one of my favorite question books by Hal Gregersen: *www.amazon.com/Questions-Are-Answer-Breakthrough-Approach/dp/0062844768*

▧ The quality of our questions determines the quality of our answers. Here's another of my favorite books on inquiry by Berger: *www.amazon.com/More-Beautiful-Question-Inquiry-Breakthrough/dp/1632861054*

▧ For a thorough introduction to the Socratic method and to elevate the depth of your discourse, review Ward Farnsworth's work: *www.amazon.com/Socratic-Method-Practitioners-Handbook/dp/1567926851*

▧ My mom tells me I've been asking questions since I was two, and I haven't stopped since! Read this favorite *HBR* article by Brooks and John: *hbr.org/2018/05/the-surprising-power-of-questions*

## Team Dynamics

▧ Reference Chapter 2's curated learning resources under "Working Together" Management System

▧ There's an element of the golden versus platinum rule underlying selfish versus selfless advocacy: *www.inc.com/peter-economy/how-the-platinum-rule-trumps-the-golden-rule-every-time.html*

▧ Teams go through Tuckman's group development model stages. Review the CliffsNotes version here: *www.*

*businessballs.com/team-management/tuckman-forming-
storming-norming-performing-model*

## chapter 7

### Communicating Nonverbally & Listening

▣ Believe it or not, researchers knew *sixty-five* years ago that
people really didn't hear or listen well to one another—so
why haven't we gotten any better since then? To learn
more, read this 1957 (not a typo!) *HBR* classic article: *hbr.
org/1957/09/listening-to-people*

▣ To learn how coaches use active listening, read this excellent
blog by ALCN Founder Helen Attridge: *nlp-leadership-
coaching.com/understanding-the-three-levels-of-listening*

▣ So much of our communication is sent through facial
expressions and nonverbal communication. For a
fascinating look at Ekman's facial expression work,
check out Dr. Vyvyan Evans' article series: *www.
psychologytoday.com/us/blog/language-in-the-mind/202001/
how-does-communication-work*

▣ We prefer communicating emotional messages
nonverbally. Read psychologist Michael Argyle's book:
*www.taylorfrancis.com/books/mono/10.4324/9780203753835/
bodily-communication-michael-argyle*

### Emotional Intelligence & Empathy

▣ To read Garg's verbatim letter to employees after the mass
Zoom firing, go to the following site: *cdn.brandfolder.io/*

*A8SA0YBW/at/ggkbfpsbjbvc335cprpv33bg/A_Message_From_ Our_Founder__CEO.pdf*

- If you're ready to level up your empathy quotient, check out cognitive, emotional, and compassionate empathy at Mind Tools: *www.mindtools.com/community/pages/article/ EmpathyatWork.php*

- If you're an executive coach seeking to expand your relationship building capacity, learn which of the twelve EI competencies clients view as critical in my PhD dissertation: *drjennifernash.com*

- If you're a Human Leader ready to level up EI, read about the twelve EI competencies in Goleman and Boyatzis's *HBR* article: *hbr.org/2017/02/emotional-intelligence-has-12- elements-which-do-you-need-to-work-on*

- I *loved* Marc Brackett's groundbreaking book *Permission to Feel*. It paints a compelling picture of why early childhood emotion education is so critical: *www.marcbrackett.com/ about/book-permission-to-feel*

- Use Yale's Mood Meter app to expand your emotional vocabulary and practice naming your emotions: *moodmeterapp.com*

- Human Leaders understand emotional contagion happens in milliseconds and why self-regulation matters. Read ScienceDirect's perspective: *www.sciencedirect.com/topics/ psychology/emotional-contagion*

- To learn more about Charles Darwin's groundbreaking work in *The Expression of Emotion in Man and Animals,* access Gutenberg's free ebook: *www.gutenberg.org/files/1227/1227-h/1227-h.htm*

### Understanding & Perspective

▪ With thirty-seven countries stamped in my passport, traveling the world and talking with people is one of my favorite ways of expanding my understanding of people, places, and things. The children's fables and folktales: *www.blessedbeyondadoubt.com/70-folktales-and-fables-from-around-the-world* and *global-geography.org/af/Geography/Asia/Cambodia/Special_Information/The_Origin_of_the_Tiger* offer perspective on other contexts, traditions, and cultural norms

▪ For eight inspiring ideas on how to better understand people, read this: *inspiringtips.com/ways-to-be-a-more-understanding-person*

▪ Read my friend and REx colleague Ludmila Praslova's deeply personal *HBR* article on neurodiversity: *hbr.org/2021/12/autism-doesnt-hold-people-back-at-work-discrimination-does*

▪ Heidi Grant highlights five shortcuts our brains take to form perceptions about others in her *HBR* article: *hbr.org/2015/04/were-all-terrible-at-understanding-each-other*

▪ Watch and listen to Deepa Purushothaman, a friend and REx colleague, discuss her personal experience as a woman of color in business: *youtu.be/9JU8ZEzfWU*. Or read *The First, The Few, The Only* at *www.amazon.com/First-Few-Only-Redefine-Corporate/dp/0063084716*

▪ Learning a language is an excellent way to gain perspective and understanding of another culture. I prefer diving in feet first by living in the country, but if that's not quite your style, try *www.rosettastone.com* or *www.babbel.com*

## chapter 8

### Art

▣ For an intriguing description of "wabi-sabi" and seeing perfection in the imperfect, check out this cultural journey through Japanese aesthetics from Lucy Dayman: *theculturetrip.com/asia/japan/articles/wabi-sabi-the-japanese-art-of-finding-perfection-in-the-imperfect*

▣ Koren's beautiful interpretation of "wabi-sabi" will delight art lovers, philosophers, and anyone with a hankering to paint gold foil on objects: *www.amazon.com/Wabi-Sabi-Artists-Designers-Poets-Philosophers/dp/0981484603*

▣ If you ever played with an Etch A Sketch as a kid, you know how difficult it is to make any sketch look good on that toy— let alone one of artistic value that matters. While researching for this book, I happened across *the* Etch A Sketch master— Jane Labowitch, aka Princess Etch. To view her amazing works of art, take a peek at her Instagram, *@PrincessEtch*

▣ For more on Princess Etch, here's an awesome *Chicago* magazine article on her: *www.chicagomag.com/arts-culture/february-2017/etch-a-sketch-princess*. Read about her designs in a *HuffPost* article celebrating Etch A Sketch's fifty-third anniversary: *www.huffpost.com/entry/etch-a-sketch-anniversary_n_3581395*

### Engagement

▣ A must-read on why engagement is low and how to better engage and keep your talent, *Gallup*'s 2021 state of the workforce survey is not to be missed: *www.gallup.com/ workplace/349484/state-of-the-global-workplace.aspx*

### Mattering

- Get a copy of *How People Matter* by Isaac Prilleltensky and Ora Prilleltensky for an excellent resource on mattering: *www.amazon.com/How-People-Matter-Affects-Happiness/ dp/1108969240*
- To learn how authoritarianism and nationalism help people feel they matter in times of uncertainty, read Fathali Moghaddam's *Threat to Democracy: The Appeal of Authoritarianism in an Age of Uncertainty*: *www.amazon.com/ Threat-Democracy-Appeal-Authoritarianism-Uncertainty/ dp/1433830701*

## chapter 9

### Appreciation Gap

- Research shows Americans have a lot of work to do to get better at expressing gratitude. Read Templeton's *The Science of Gratitude*: *www.templeton.org/wp-content/ uploads/2018/05/Gratitude_whitepaper_fnl.pdf*

### Gratitude

- For additional ideas on how to show gratitude at work, review Center for Creative Leadership's list: *www.ccl.org/ articles/leading-effectively-articles/giving-thanks-will-make-you-a-better-leader*

- For yet more ideas on workplace gratitude, check out NBC's suggestions: *www.nbcnews.com/better/business/5-signs-you-re-appreciated-work-what-do-if-you-ncna821816*

- You're not alone if you haven't seen gratitude at work. Sue Shellenbarger explains how commonplace this is, unfortunately: *www.wsj.com/articles/SB100014241278873243 52004578131002460783008*

- If you haven't seen the classic movie *Office Space*, here are options for viewing: *www.imdb.com/title/tt0151804*. NB: Red stapler not included

- O.C. Tanner's research suggests that when employees are appreciated and recognized for their great work, they become more loyal, committed, and engaged: *www. octanner.com/global-culture-report.html*

- Here are additional ideas for appreciation and gratitude in the workplace from Schwartz: *hbr.org/2012/01/why-appreciation-matters-so-mu.html*

- If you want to write a handwritten note of appreciation, but your penmanship or Hallmark skills come up short, there are many ideas available online; Google "online cards" and "what to say in an appreciation card" for writing thought-starters

- For breathing exercises designed to calm the nervous system and support gratitude, read my thoughts here: *thriveglobal.com/stories/the-power-of-gratitude-6*

### Leadership & Follower Health

- Every leader should read this evidence-based study on how their actions (or lack thereof) may negatively impact follower health: *www.researchgate.net/publication/ 254202070_The_impact_of_leadership_on_the_health_of_ subordinates*

### Neuroscience of Gratitude

- For the neuroscience of giving thanks (fascinating stuff!), read Korb's take on prefrontal nudity—the cortex kind: *www.psychologytoday.com/us/blog/prefrontal-nudity/201211/ the-grateful-brain*
- If you don't show gratitude often, you're not alone. Allen's article explains why it may be harder for you than others: *greatergood.berkeley.edu/article/item/why_is_gratitude_so_hard_ for_some_people*
- Expressing appreciation or gratitude releases oxytocin— the social interaction glue responsible for strengthening relationships. This study offers insights: *academic.oup.com/ scan/article/9/12/1855/1611597*
- Research shows gratitude makes people happier and healthier. Find Templeton's online gratitude journal experiment results: *greatergood.berkeley.edu/article/item/a_ thnx_a_day_keeps_the_doctor_away*

## chapter 10

### Authentic Leadership

- To learn more about authentic leadership development, get a copy of Avolio and Gardner's article titled "Authentic leadership development: Getting to the root of positive forms of leadership": *www.sciencedirect.com/science/article/pii/S1048984305000263*

### Bhopal Disaster Relief

- Contributions to the Bhopal Medical Appeal can be made: *www.bhopal.org*

### Failure of Borders and Eastman Kodak

- To learn from the past, peruse these timeless examples of Kodak and Borders:
    - *hbr.org/2016/07/kodaks-downfall-wasnt-about-technology*
    - *www.npr.org/2011/07/19/138514209/why-borders-failed-while-barnes-and-noble-survived*
    - *business.time.com/2011/07/19/5-reasons-borders-went-out-of-business-and-what-will-take-its-place/*

### Inspiration Judo

- When you have problem employees who need motivation, read Nigel Nicholson's perspective here: *hbr.org/2003/01/how-to-motivate-your-problem-people*
- It's not just leaders who have to learn how to inspire others. Artistic souls also go through the same learning curve. Learn more: *www.arts.gov/sites/default/files/nea_arts/NEA_ARTS4_2013.pdf*
- Read Bain & Company's perspective: *www.bain.com/insights/how-leaders-inspire-cracking-the-code*

### Inspiring Communication

▫ Words do make a difference. Read Joel Schwartzberg's thoughts on how to shape your language to inspire others: *hbr.org/2021/04/find-the-right-words-to-inspire-your-team*

▫ For inspiration military style, get some popcorn and watch Patton's speech in the movie *Patton* on YouTube: *youtu.be/PS5yfhPGaWE*

### Nightbirde Foundation

▫ Jane's family set up the Nightbirde Foundation to bring hope and healing to young women with breast cancer. Learn more, get involved, or donate: *www.nightbirdefoundation.org/take-action*

### Storytelling

▫ Presenter Akash Karia shares twenty-three proven techniques from TED Talks to build your storytelling prowess in his book: *www.amazon.com/TED-Talks-Storytelling-Techniques-Best/dp/1507503008*

▫ From master storyteller David Hutchens, here are best practices of the world's most influential story consultants and knowledge workers: *www.amazon.com/Circle-Muses-Storytelling-Innovators-Meaning/dp/1118973968*

▫ If you like listening rather than reading, then *The Moth Radio Hour* is for you: *themoth.org/radio-hour*

▫ Read *TED Talks: The Official TED Guide to Public Speaking* by TED curator Chris Anderson, to get better at storytelling: *www.ted.com/read/ted-talks-the-official-ted-guide-to-public-speaking*

▣ Watch Nightbirde's inspiring, tear-inducing, golden-buzzer winning *AGT* audition here: *youtu.be/CZJvBfoHDk0*

### Trust—Take Two

▣ Here is another trust model from Great Places to Work: *www.greatplacetowork.com/trust-model*
▣ My friend and REx colleague Ron Carucci's book on developing trust and ethical leadership should be on every leader's list: *www.amazon.com/Be-Honest-Power-Justice-Purpose-ebook/dp/B091V7BFZY*
▣ For more on the Trust Quotient instrument, read this: *trustedadvisor.com/public/Trusted-Advisors_TQ-Assessment_What-You-Need-to-Know_1-10-18.pdf.* Or watch this: *trustedadvisor.com/why-trust-matters/understanding-trust/understanding-the-trust-equation*

### Vision

▣ For a light-hearted yet substantive look at vision, read David Hutchens's *The Lemming Dilemma: Living with Purpose, Leading with Vision*: *https://www.amazon.com/dp/B005PQIE5M*

## chapter 11

### Belonging, Mortality, and Social Interaction

▣ For a fascinating look at how humans became social, read Elizabeth Pennisi's article: *www.science.org/content/article/how-humans-became-social*

▨ To learn what buffers against mortality, watch psychiatrist Robert Waldinger's TED Talk on lessons from Harvard's eighty-year-long happiness study: *www.youtube.com/ watch?v=8KkKuTCFvzI*

### Dehumanizing & Ignoring

▨ NPR interviews David Smith about his book *Less Than Human: Why We Demean, Enslave, and Exterminate Others*: *www.npr.org/2011/03/29/134956180/ criminals-see-their-victims-as-less-than-human*

▨ Nicholas Epley shares his perspectives on how humans are denied their humanity: *www.salon.com/2014/03/02/the_ psychology_of_hate_how_we_deny_human_beings_their_humanity*

▨ I first learned about Zimbardo's Stanford prison experiment during my MBA program. It was so disturbing, it made me physically ill, and I had to leave the room during the film: *www.prisonexp.org*

▨ For more on how meaningless office speak and jargon came into being at work, starting with Taylor's dehumanizing people as machines, read this: *www. theatlantic.com/business/archive/2014/04/business-speak/ 361135*

▨ Ignoring others is at our own peril. Read Margaret Heffernan's book titled *Willful Blindness* for more insights: *www.amazon.com/Willful-Blindness-Ignore-Obvious-Peril/ dp/0802777961*

### Detroit

- Go here to find out how you can watch *8 Mile* featuring Eminem and his music: *www.imdb.com/title/tt0298203/*
- Find the *8 Mile* soundtrack at Shady Records: *www.shadyrecords.com/album/8-mile*
- Tommey Walker is founder of Detroit vs Everybody, a clothing company showcasing Detroit's pride and unapologetic spirit: *vseverybody.com*
- This NBC News special highlights the story of Detroit's dividing "Birwood Wall": *www.nbcnews.com/specials/detroit-segregation-wall*

### Inclusion & Dance

- I admit I'm obsessed with my Peloton workouts, and Alex is one of my favorite instructors. Nearly all of my personal bests have been on his watch because of his inspirational (and hard-core!) style. Watch Carson Daly interview (and then workout with) Alex on *Today* here: *www.today.com/video/meet-carson-daly-s-inspiring-peloton-instructor-alex-toussaint-99516485888*
- For McKinsey's perspective on inclusion, review their research here: *www.mckinsey.com/business-functions/people-and-organizational-performance/our-insights/understanding-organizational-barriers-to-a-more-inclusive-workplace*
- *HBR* shares thinking on human moments at work: *hbr.org/1999/01/the-human-moment-at-work*
- Watch *Dancing in Jaffa* starring Pierre Dulaine: *www.imdb.com/title/tt2125480*

▨ Enjoy Pierre's TED talk on his dance journey in Jaffa: *youtu.be/eR8YlpqA2nA*

### Mirroring

▨ The mirroring strategy applies to everything in life. Watch Chris Voss's perspective here: *www.youtube.com/watch?v=llctqNJr2IU*

### Neuroscience & Biases

▨ My friend and REx community founder Dorie Clark shares how to see people as they really are: *www.forbes.com/sites/dorieclark/2015/04/14/how-to-see-people-as-they-really-are/?sh=58632e8170ab*

▨ To learn more about the primacy effect in psychology, this article from Verywell Mind is a great start: *www.verywellmind.com/understanding-the-primacy-effect-4685243*

▨ Gaining awareness of your biases is the first step to changing your behavior. *HBR* has some excellent suggestions to get started: *hbr.org/2022/02/ascend-2-8-are-you-aware-of-your-biases*

▨ Remember the macaque monkey study that imitated the researcher's behavior? Read about mirror neurons here: *citeseerx.ist.psu.edu/viewdoc/download?doi=10.1.1.553.2582&rep=rep1&type=pdf*

# chapter 12

## Divergent Thinking

- Read *Listening to the Volcano: Conversations That Open Our Minds to New Possibilities* from Hutchens: *www.amazon.com/Listening-Volcano-Conversations-Possibilities-Learning-ebook/dp/B007RG691Y*
- Cognitive diversity isn't just for brainstorming; it guards against groupthink and boosts diversity and inclusion. Read Deloitte's perspective: *www2.deloitte.com/us/en/insights/topics/talent/diversitys-new-frontier.html*

## Goals & Success

- Behavior-based goals take SMART goals to the next level. Read this article to learn more: *your.yale.edu/its-important-set-behavioral-goals*
- Elevating others helps you and them succeed. Read perspectives from me and six Recognized Expert colleagues: *www.linkedin.com/pulse/s%C3%AD-se-puede-jennifer-nash-phd-she-her-*
- Many leaders don't take the time to celebrate goal achievement, which is critical to success. Read Carmody's thoughts: *www.inc.com/bill-carmody/3-reasons-celebrating-your-many-accomplishments-is-critical-to-your-success.html*

# notes

## Introduction

1   To listen to this audio message, please go to *drjennifernash.com/ behumanleadhuman/mulally*.

## Chapter 1

1   Jacob Morgan, *The Future of Work*, 1st Edition (New York: Wiley, 2014).

2   Hugh Son and Dawn Giel, "Jamie Dimon, Fed Up with Zoom Calls and Remote Work, Says Commuting to Offices Will Make a Comeback," CNBC, May 4, 2021, https://www.cnbc. com/2021/05/04/jamie-dimon-fed-up-with-zoom-calls-and-remote-work-says-commuting-to-offices-will-make-a-comeback.html.

3   Jeanne Sahadi, "90% of Employers Say Working Remotely Hasn't Hurt Productivity," CNN Business, August 27, 2020, https://www. cnn.com/2020/08/27/success/work-from-home-employer-plans-for-more-flexible-policies/index.html.

4   Kathryn Dill, "WeWork CEO Says Least Engaged Employees Enjoy Working From Home," *The Wall Street Journal*, May 12, 2021, https:// www.wsj.com/articles/wework-ceo-says-workers-who-want-back-into-the-office-are-the-most-engaged-11620837018.

5    Vicky McKeever, "Goldman Sachs CEO Solomon Calls Working from Home an 'Aberration,'" CNBC, February 25, 2021, https://www.cnbc.com/2021/02/25/goldman-sachs-ceo-solomon-calls-working-from-home-an-aberration-.html.

6    Best Practice Institute, "Over 83% of CEOs Want Employees Back in the Office in 2021, Only 10% of Employees Want to Return Full Time According to New Best Practice Institute Study," press release, December 29, 2020, https://www.prweb.com/releases/over_83_of_ceos_want_employees_back_in_the_office_in_2021_only_10_of_employees_want_to_return_full_time_according_to_new_best_practice_institute_study/prweb17632252.htm.

7    Thomas Mahan et al., "2020 Retention Report: Insights on 2019 Turnover Trends, Reasons, Costs & Recommendations" (Franklin, TN: Work Institute, 2020), https://workinstitute.com/retention-report.

8    World Economic Forum Platform for Shaping the Future of the New Economy and Society, "The Future of Jobs Report: 2020," World Economic Forum, October 2020, https://www3.weforum.org/docs/WEF_Future_of_Jobs_2020.pdf.

9    David Hockney, interview with the author, January 27, 2022.

10   Allana Akhtar, "A CEO Who Writes 9,200 Employee Holiday Cards a Year Explains the Value of Gratitude," *Insider*, December 24, 2019, https://www.businessinsider.com/ceo-writes-7400-employee-birthday-cards-each-year-2017-6.

### Chapter 2

1    Alan Mulally, interview with the author, August 14, 2019.

2    Business Roundtable, "Statement on the Purpose of a Corporation," August 19, 2019, https://opportunity.businessroundtable.org/ourcommitment/.

3    Douglas A. Ready et al., "The New Leadership Playbook for the Digital Age: Reimagining What It Takes to Lead," 2020 Future of Leadership Global Executive Study and Research Report, January 21, 2020, https://sloanreview.mit.edu/projects/the-new-leadership-playbook-for-the-digital-age/.

4    Mulally, interview.

5   Alan Mulally, "A Conversation with Alan Mulally About His 'Working Together'© Strategic, Operational, and Stakeholder-Centered Management System," interview by Sarah McArthur, Leader to Leader 2022, no. 104 (January 27, 2022), https://doi.org/10.1002/ltl.20628.

6   Laura Ilona Urrila, "From Personal Wellbeing to Relationships: A Systematic Review on the Impact of Mindfulness Interventions and Practices on Leaders," *Human Resource Management Review* 32, no. 3 (2021): 100837, https://doi.org/10.1016/j.hrmr.2021.100837.

7   Kim Cameron, Carlos Mora, Trevor Leutscher, Margaret Calarco, "Effects of Positive Practices on Organizational Effectiveness," *The Journal of Applied Behavioral Science* 47, no. 3 (August 2011): 266–308, https://doi.org/10.1177/0021886310395514.

8   Daniel Goleman, Richard Boyatzis, and Annie McKee, *Primal Leadership, with a New Preface by the Authors: Unleashing the Power of Emotional Intelligence* (Cambridge, MA: Harvard Business Review Press, 2013).

9   Akhtar, "A CEO Who Writes 9,200 Employee Holiday Cards a Year."

10  Olivia Croom, interview with the author, July 11, 2019.

11  Business Roundtable, "Statement on the Purpose of a Corporation."

12  Jennifer A. Nash, "Developmental Factors Influencing Effective Leaders: A Life Story View of Executive Leadership Development," in *Research on Emotions in Organizations (Vol. 15): Emotions and Leadership*, eds. Neal M. Ashkanasy, Wilfred J. Zerbe, and Charmine E. J. Härtel (Emerald Publishing Limited, 2019), 243.

13  Ram Charan, Dominic Barton, and Dennis Carey, *Talent Wins: The New Playbook for Putting People First* (Cambridge, MA: Harvard Business Review Press, 2018) p. 3.

14  Jennifer Nash quoted in Ludmila Praslova's post, "WORK 3.0—the Vision for Post-Pandemic Work. Part 2: Leadership 3.0," LinkedIn, December 20, 2020, https://www.linkedin.com/pulse/work-30-vision-post-pandemic-part-2-leadership-ludmila/.

### Chapter 3

1   Kerri Walsh Jennings, "On Her Turf: Athletes' Mindset," interview with NBC Olympics, clip at 1:34–2:17, accessed August 1, 2021,

https://www.nbcolympics.com/videos/kerri-walsh-jennings-talks-fairy-tale-olympics-experiences.

2    Robert K. Greenleaf, *Servant Leadership: A Journey into the Nature of Legitimate Power and Greatness* (New Jersey: Paulist Press, 1977), 33.

3    Giada Di Stefano, Francesca Gino, Gary P. Pisano, Bradley R. Staats, "Making Experience Count: The Role of Reflection in Individual Learning," Harvard Business School NOM Unit Working Paper No. 14-093, Harvard Business School Technology & Operations Mgt. Unit Working Paper No. 14-093, HEC Paris Research Paper No. SPE-2016-1181 (June 2016), http://dx.doi.org/10.2139/ssrn.2414478.

4    Jennifer Nash, "What Are Your Personal Values," *Harvard Business Review*, November 26, 2020, https://hbr.org/2020/11/what-are-your-personal-values.

5    Brendan Cole, "Seven-Year-Old Girl Raises Hundreds of Dollars for Animals Devastated by Australian Wildfires by Selling Juice," *Newsweek*, January 14, 2020, https://www.newsweek.com/wildfires-australia-animals-injured-english-girl-1482061.

6    Marcus Buckingham, *Go Put Your Strengths to Work: 6 Powerful Steps to Achieve Outstanding Performance* (New York: Simon & Schuster, 2007).

7    Access the CliftonStrengths assessment at: https://www.gallup.com/cliftonstrengths/en/252137/home.aspx.

8    Access the CareerLeader assessment at: https://www.careerleader.com/Program.

9    Access the VIA Character Strengths assessment at: https://www.viacharacter.org.

10   Access the ESCI assessment at: https://www.kornferry.com/capabilities/leadership-professional-development/training-certification/esci-emotional-and-social-competency-inventory.

11   Mihaly Csikszentmihalyi passed away while I was writing this chapter in 2021. RIP Mihaly. Flow description and concept derived from Mihaly Csikszentmihalyi, "Flow, the Secret to Happiness," TEDTalk, February 2004, video, https://www.ted.com/talks/mihaly_csikszentmihalyi_flow_the_secret_to_happiness; Mihaly Csikszentmihalyi, Flow: The Psychology of Optimal Experience (New York: Harper Perennial, 1990).

12    Vinoth K. Ranganathan et al., "From Mental Power to Muscle
      Power—Gaining Strength by Using the Mind," *Neuropsychologia*
      42, no. 7 (2004): 944–956, https://doi.org/10.1016/j.
      neuropsychologia.2003.11.018; Radu Predoiu et al., "Visualisation
      Techniques in Sport—The Mental Road Map for Success," *Physical
      Education, Sport, and Kinetotherapy Journal* 59, no. 3 (2020): 245–256,
      https://doi.org/10.35189/dpeskj.2020.59.3.4; Thomas Newmark, "Cases
      in Visualization for Improved Athletic Performance," *Psychiatric Annals*
      42, no. 10 (2012): 385, https://doi.org/10.3928/00485713-20121003-07.

## Chapter 4

1     Geneva Williams, interview with the author, July 9, 2019.
2     Priscilla, interview with the author, June 18, 2019.
3     Vauhini Telikapalli, interview with the author, January 7, 2020.
4     Graham, interview with the author, June 27, 2019.
5     Manny Ocasio, interview with the author, September 18, 2019.
6     Bill Gryzenia, interview with the author, August 6, 2019.
7     Edgar H. Schein and Peter A. Schein, *Humble Leadership: The Power
      of Relationships, Openness, and Trust* (Oakland, CA: Berrett-Koehler
      Publishing, 2018).
8     Nancy Baym, Jonathan Larson, and Ronnie Marin, "What a Year
      of WFH Has Done to Our Relationships at Work," *Harvard Business
      Review*, March 22, 2021, https://hbr.org/2021/03/what-a-year-of-
      wfh-has-done-to-our-relationships-at-work.
9     Dorie Clark, "The Real Reason You Feel So Busy (and What to Do
      About It)," TEDxBoston, November 2021, video, 7:47, https://www.
      ted.com/talks/dorie_clark_the_real_reason_you_feel_so_busy_and_
      what_to_do_about_it.
10    Hugh Blane, interview with the author, August 14, 2019.
11    Tarina, interview with the author, September 4, 2019.
12    Ellen, interview with the author, December 10, 2019.
13    Karl Shaikh, interview with the author, October 15, 2019.
14    Mulally, interview.
15    Adam M. Grant, *Give and Take: Why Helping Others Drives Our Success*
      (New York: Penguin Books, 2013) p. 4.

16 Olivia Croom, interview with the author, July 11, 2019.

17 Blane, interview.

18 Bruce D. Perry and Maia Szalavitz, *The Boy Who Was Raised as a Dog: And Other Stories from a Child Psychiatrist's Notebook—What Traumatized Children Can Teach Us About Loss, Love, and Healing* (New York: Basic Books, 2017).

## Chapter 5

1 Online Etymology Dictionary, s.v. "relation," accessed June 2, 2022, https://www.etymonline.com/word/relation.

2 Jennifer Nash, "The Power of Relationships: Navigating the Dance of Change through Executive Coaching" (dissertation, Case Western Reserve University, 2018), https://drjennifernash.com/resources/.

## Chapter 6

1 Ingrid Tolentino, interview with the author, September 18, 2019

2 Alan Mulally, interview with the author, August 14, 2019

3 Ford Media Center, "Ford Achieves 2014 Pre-Tax Profit of $6.3 Billion, Net Income of $3.2 Billion; 2015 Outlook for Pre-Tax Profit at $8.5 Billion to $9.5 Billion," press release, January 29, 2015, https://media.ford.com/content/fordmedia/fna/us/en/news/2015/01/29/4qfinancials.html.

4 Akhtar, "WeWork's CEO."

5 Simon Thomsen, "The Expression 'Drinking the Kool-Aid' Was Coined from a Horrifying Tragedy That Happened 40 Years Ago This Weekend," *Insider Australia*, November 16, 2018, https://www.businessinsider.com/drinking-the-kool-aid-meaning-jonestown-massacre-2018-11.

6 Tarina, interview with the author, September 4, 2019.

7 The graphic with this information, https://www.politifact.com/2020/, has since been deactivated, but for more information direct inquiries to truthometer@politifact.com.

8 Allie Shobe, interview with the author, September 12, 2019.

9 Shobe, interview.

10    Barbara Gray, "How to Fact Check Like a Pro: 10 Tips for Fighting
      Fake News," LexisNexis, accessed June 3, 2022, http://www.
      lexisnexis.com/pdf/nexis/Nexis-webinar-how-to-fact-check-like-a-
      pro.pdf.

11    David Craig, interview with the author, December 3, 2019.

## Chapter 7

1     Shobe, interview.

2     Ralph G. Nichols, "The Struggle to Be Human" (keynote address,
      First Annual Convention of the International Listening Association,
      Atlanta, GA, February 17, 1980), https://listen.org/resources/
      Documents/Nichols%20Struggle%20to%20be%20Human.pdf.

3     Shira Miller, interview with the author, May 30, 2019.

4     Stephen R. Covey, *The 7 Habits of Highly Effective People, 30th
      Anniversary Edition* (New York: Simon & Schuster, 2020) p. 298.

5     Derrick Bryson Taylor and Jenny Gross, "The Better.com CEO Says
      He's 'Deeply Sorry' for Firing Workers Over Zoom," *The New York
      Times*, December 8, 2021, https://www.nytimes.com/2021/12/08/
      business/better-zoom-layoffs-vishal-garg.html.

6     Maxwell Strachan, "Better CEO 'Taking Time Off Effective
      Immediately': Email," *Vice*, December 10, 2021, https://www.vice.
      com/en/article/jgmpab/better-ceo-taking-time-off-effective-
      immediately-email.

7     Emma Goldberg, "Better.com's CEO Is 'Taking Time Off' After
      Firing 900 Workers Over Zoom," *The New York Times*, December 10,
      2021, https://www.nytimes.com/2021/12/10/business/economy/
      better-ceo-zoom-firing.html.

8     David Jeans and Noah Kirsch, "Mortgages, Fraud Claims, and
      'Dumb Dolphins': A Tangled Past Haunts Better.com CEO Vishal
      Garg," *Forbes*, November 20, 2020, https://www.forbes.com/sites/
      davidjeans/2020/11/20/mortgages-fraud-claims-and-dumb-
      dolphins-a-tangled-past-haunts-bettercom-ceo-vishal-garg.

9     Jessi Hempel, "LinkedIn Top Startups 2020: The 50 US Companies on
      the Rise," LinkedIn, September 22, 2020, https://www.linkedin.com/
      pulse/linkedin-top-startups-2020-50-us-companies-rise-jessi-hempel.

10   Dan Primack, "Better.com Delays Close of $7.7B Reverse Merger After Mass Layoffs," *Axios*, December 8, 2021, https://www.axios.com/2021/12/08/better-home-mortgage-delays-reverse-merger-layoffs.

11   *Breaking Bad*, season 3, episode 6, "Sunset," directed and written by John Shiban, aired April 25, 2010, Sony Pictures Home Entertainment.

12   Daniel Goleman, *Emotional Intelligence: Why It Can Matter More Than IQ* (New York: Random House, 1995).

13   Matthew D. Lieberman et al., "Putting Feelings Into Words," *Psychological Science* 18, no. 5 (2007): 421–428, https://doi.org/10.1111/j.1467-9280.2007.01916.x.

14   Douglas Heingartner, "Now Hear This, Quickly," *The New York Times*, October 2, 2003, https://www.nytimes.com/2003/10/02/technology/now-hear-this-quickly.html.

15   Albert Mehrabian, *Silent Messages: Implicit Communication of Emotions and Attitudes*, 2nd Edition (Belmont, CA: Wadsworth Publishing Co, 1980).

16   Charles Dawin, *The Expression of the Emotions of Man and Animals* (London: John Murray, 1872).

17   Michael Argyle, *Bodily Communication* (New York: Routledge, 2010).

18   Ann, interview with the author, October 1, 2019.

19   Chesley B. Sullenberger III, *Sully: My Search for What Really Matters* (New York: William Morrow, 2016).

20   Accenture, "Accenture Research Finds Listening More Difficult in Today's Digital Workplace," press release, Februrary 26, 2015, https://newsroom.accenture.com/industries/global-media-industry-analyst-relations/accenture-research-finds-listening-more-difficult-in-todays-digital-workplace.htm.

21   Bob Sullivan and Hugh Thompson, "Now Hear This! Most People Stink at Listening," *Scientific American*, May 3, 2013, https://www.scientificamerican.com/article/plateau-effect-digital-gadget-distraction-attention/, excerpted from *The Plateau Effect: Getting from Stuck to Success* (New York: Dutton, 2013).

22   Sullivan and Thompson, "Now Hear This!"

23   Joel Tauber, interview with the author, December 3, 2019.

24 Adam D. Galinsky et al., "Why It Pays to Get Inside the Head of Your Opponent: The Differential Effects of Perspective Taking and Empathy in Negotiations," *Psychological Science* 19, no. 4 (2008): 378–384, https://doi.org/10.1111/j.1467-9280.2008.02096.x.

25 Daniel Goleman, "What Makes a Leader," *Harvard Business Review* (January 2004), https://hbr.org/2004/01/what-makes-a-leader.

26 Goleman, *Emotional Intelligence.*

27 Goleman, *Emotional Intelligence.*

28 Brené Brown, *Atlas of the Heart* (New York: Harper Collins, 2021) p. xxi.

29 Interactive Plutchik's Wheel of Emotions available at: https://www.6seconds.org/2022/03/13/plutchik-wheel-emotions.

30 1980s research by Susan Fiske and Shelly Taylor, cited in Heidi Grant, "We're All Terrible at Understanding Each Other," *Harvard Business Review*, April 16, 2015, https://hbr.org/2015/04/were-all-terrible-at-understanding-each-other.

31 Mulally, interview.

32 Bryce G. Hoffman, *American Icon: Alan Mulally and the Fight to Save Ford Motor Company* (New York: Crown Business, 2012) p. 103.

33 Gops Gopaluni, interview with the author, August 9, 2019.

### Chapter 8

1 Tricia Burger, interview with the author, September 4, 2019.

2 Gregory Elliott, *Family Matters: The Importance of Mattering to Family in Adolescence* (Malden, MA: Wiley-Blackwell, 2009), 339.

3 Eleonora Manuel, interview with the author, June 21, 2019.

4 The Associated Press, "Key Moments Surrounding Michigan High School Shooting," AP News, December 4, 2021, https://apnews.com/article/crime-shootings-education-michigan-school-shootings-a734bfa163d0e761b1eac3031ba0569a.

5 Mark R. Leary et al., "Teasing, Rejection, and Violence: Case Studies of the School Shootings," *Aggressive Behavior* 29, no. 3 (April 2003): 202–214, https://doi.org/10.1002/ab.10061.

6 "Amanda Gorman: Uplifting Literacy," We the Future: Young Leaders of Social Change, online exhibit by the Bill and Melinda

Gates Foundation Discovery Center, accessed June 4, 2022, https://www.discovergates.org/exhibition/wethefuture/young-leaders/amanda-gorman.

7   *Gallup, State of the Global Workplace: 2021 Report*, accessed June 4, 2022, https://www.gallup.com/workplace/349484/state-of-the-global-workplace.aspx.

8   Isaac Prilleltensky and Ora Prilleltensky, *How People Matter: Why It Affects Health, Happiness, Love, Work, and Society* (Cambridge, UK: Cambridge University Press, 2021) p. 4.

9   Fathali M. Moghaddam, *Threat to Democracy: The Appeal of Authoritarianism in an Age of Uncertainty* (American Psychological Association, 2019).

10   Robin DiAngelo, *White Fragility: Why It's So Hard for White People to Talk About Racism* (New York: Penguin, 2018).

11   Leonard Koren, *Wabi-Sabi for Artists, Designers, Poets & Philosophers* (Berkeley, CA: Stone Bridge Press, 2008), p. 26.

12   "Weaving a Spirit Pathway," Less than Perfect, accessed July 13, 2022, https://exhibitions.kelsey.lsa.umich.edu/less-than-perfect/navajo.php.

13   Telikapalli, interview.

14   Franco Girimonte, interview with the author, July 24, 2019.

15   Tony Schwartz, "Why Appreciation Matters So Much," *Harvard Business Review*, January 23, 2012, https://hbr.org/2012/01/why-appreciation-matters-so-mu.html.

16   Christine Espinosa, interview with the author, July 15, 2020.

17   G. Richard Shell, "Improve Your Influence: Build Stronger Rapport," Wharton@Work Nano Tools for Leaders, September 2016, https://executiveeducation.wharton.upenn.edu/thought-leadership/wharton-at-work/2016/09/improve-your-influence.

18   Tarina, interview.

19   Wayne Baker and Jane E. Dutton, "Enabling Positive Social Capital in Organizations," in *Exploring Positive Relationships at Work: Building a Theoretical and Research Foundation*, eds. Jane E. Dutton and Belle Rose Ragins (Lawrence Erlbaum, Inc., 2006) p. 325–345.

20   Kim Cameron, Jane E. Dutton, and Robert E. Quinn, "An Introduction to Positive Organizational Scholarship," in *Positive*

*Organizational Scholarship: Foundations of a New Discipline* (San Francisco: Berrett-Koehler, 2003) p. 4.

## Chapter 9

1    Marilyn Asahi, interview with the author, April 1, 2021.

2    Hawaiʻi Law of The Aloha Spirit, §5-7.5 (1986), https://www.hawaii.edu/uhwo/clear/home/lawaloha.html.

3    R.A. Emmons and M.E. McCollough, "Counting Blessings versus Burdens: An Experimental Investigation of Gratitude and Subjective Well-Being in Daily Life," *Journal of Personality and Social Psychology* 84, no. 2 (2003): 377–389, https://doi.org/10.1037/0022-3514.84.2.377.

4    Michael Mawson, "Parade Celebrates Area's First Responders," Bennington Banner, June 20, 2021, https://www.benningtonbanner.com/local-news/parade-celebrates-areas-first-responders/article_16e4fe0a-d1ce-11eb-83d3-1fa5408bc7ac.html.

5    Adam M. Grant and Francesca Gino, "A Little Thanks Goes a Long Way: Explaining Why Gratitude Expressions Motivate Prosocial Behavior," *Journal of Personality and Social Psychology* 98, no. 6 (June 2010): 946–955, https://doi.org/10.1037/a0017935.

6    Anna Nyberg et al., "Managerial Leadership and Ischaemic Heart Disease Among Employees: The Swedish WOLF Study," *Occupational & Environmental Medicine* 66, no. 1 (2008): 51–55, http://dx.doi.org/10.1136/oem.2008.039362.

7    Marcial Losada and Emily Heaphy, "The Role of Positivity and Connectivity in the Performance of Business Teams: A Nonlinear Dynamics Model," *American Behavioral Scientist* (February 2004): 740–765, https://doi.org/10.1177/0002764203260208.

8    Emiliana R. Simon-Thomas and Jeremy Adam Smith, "How Grateful Are Americans," *Greater Good Magazine*, January 10, 2013, https://greatergood.berkeley.edu/article/item/how_grateful_are_americans.

9    *Office Space*, directed by Mike Judge (1999; Beverly Hills, Calif: 20th Century Fox Home Entertainment).

10   Greg Iacurci, "The Great Resignation Continues, as 44% of Workers Look for a New Job," CNBC, March 22, 2022, https://www.cnbc.

com/2022/03/22/great-resignation-continues-as-44percent-of-workers-seek-a-new-job.html. For current numbers please go to https://www.bls.gov/news.release/jolts.toc.htm.

11    Miller, interview.

12    Brad Brezinski, interview with the author, June 28, 2019.

13    Damian Zikakis, interview with the author, July 11, 2019.

14    Shibeal O'Flaherty, Michael T. Sanders, and Ashley Whillans, "Research: A Little Recognition Can Provide a Big Morale Boost, *Harvard Business Review*, March 29, 2021, https://hbr.org/2021/03/research-a-little-recognition-can-provide-a-big-morale-boost.

15    Ahktar, "A CEO Who Writes 9,200 Employee Holiday Cards a Year."

16    Rodger Dean Duncan, "Close Encounters: Leadership and Handwritten Notes," *Forbes*, April 6, 2018, https://www.forbes.com/sites/rodgerdeanduncan/2018/04/06/close-encounters-leadership-and-handwritten-notes/?sh=63dcfb353e96.

17    Indra Nooyi, *My Life in Full: Work, Family, and Our Future* (Portfolio, 2021) p. 215–216.

18    Jess Evans, interviews with the author, September 5 & 10, 2019.

19    Damian Zikakis, interview with the author, July 11, 2019.

### Chapter 10

1    Brezinski, interview.

2    *Patton*, directed by Franklin J Schaffner (1970; 20th Century Fox).

3    Colette M Taylor, Casey J. Cornelius, and Kate Colvin, "Visionary Leadership and Its Relationship to Organizational Effectiveness," *Leadership & Organizational Development Journal* 35, no. 6 (August 2014): 566–583, https://doi.org/10.1108/LODJ-10-2012-0130.

4    Stuart Diamond, "The Bhopal Disaster: How It Happened," *The New York Times*, January 28, 1985, https://www.nytimes.com/1985/01/28/world/the-bhopal-disaster-how-it-happened.html.

5    *Britannica*, s.v. "Union Carbide Corporation," updated March 20, 2019, https://www.britannica.com/topic/Union-Carbide-Corporation.

6    Edward Broughton, "The Bhopal Disaster and Its Aftermath: A Review," *Environmental Health* 4, no. 6 (2005), https://doi.org/10.1186/1476-069X-4-6.

7   Sanjay Kumar, "Victims of Gas Leak in Bhopal Seek Redress on
    Compensation," *BMJ* (August 2004), https://doi.org/10.1136/
    bmj.329.7462.366-b.

8   To see Judah's additional Bhopal images, see Judah Passow, "The
    Bhopal Disaster Victims Still Waiting for Justice 35 Years On—In
    Pictures," *The Guardian*, December 7, 2019, https://www.theguardian.
    com/cities/gallery/2019/dec/07/the-bhopal-disaster-victims-still-
    waiting-for-justice-35-years-on-in-pictures.

9   To learn how you can support those affected by this disaster, visit
    www.bhopal.org.

10  Amy Anger, interview with the author, July 9, 2019.

11  Julien Rotter (1967), "A New Scale for the Measurement of
    Interpersonal Trust," *Journal of Personality* 35(4): 651, https://doi.
    org/10.1111/j.1467-6494.1967.tb01454.x.

12  Stephen M.R. Covey, "The Business Case for Trust," *Chief Executive*,
    June 4, 2007, https://chiefexecutive.net/the-business-case-for-trust.

13  Stephen M.R. Covey, "The Speed of Trust: It's a Learnable Skill,"
    interview by Rodger Dean Duncan, *Forbes*, July 12, 2018, https://
    www.forbes.com/sites/rodgerdeanduncan/2018/07/12/the-speed-of-
    trust-its-a-learnable-skill/?sh=16f193093bbf.

14  BS is an abbreviation for "bullshit". For more insight into the slang
    usage of this term, see Collins Dictionary, s.v. "bullshit," accessed
    June 7, 2022, https://www.collinsdictionary.com/us/dictionary/
    english/bullshit.

15  Oleg Konovalov, *The Vision Code: How to Create and Execute a
    Compelling Vision for Your Business* (Wiley, 2021).

16  Konovalov, *The Vision Code*, p. 142.

17  Konovalov, *The Vision Code*, p. 84.

18  TED talks available at https://www.ted.com/talks; Moth Radio Hour
    available at https://themoth.org/radio-hour.

19  Jonah Sachs, *Winning the Story Wars: Why Those Who Tell (and Live) the
    Best Stories Will Rule the Future* (Cambridge, MA: Harvard Business
    Review Press, 2012).

20  Fred O. Walumbwa et al., "Authentic Leadership: Development
    and Validation of a Theory-Based Measure," *Journal of*

*Management* 34, no. 1 (October 2007): 89–126, https://doi. org/10.1177/0149206307308913.

21  To access a free version of the leader questions, go to: https:// authenticleadershipblog.files.wordpress.com/2012/07/authentic-leadership-questionnaire.pdf. To take a fee-based, multi-rater questionnaire and receive an automated report, visit: https://www. mindgarden.com/69-authentic-leadership-questionnaire.

22  David H. Maister, Charles H. Green, and Robert M. Galford, *The Trusted Advisor* (Touchstone, 2001).

23  To access a free version of the instrument, go to: https://trustsuite. trustedadvisor.com.

24  Gopaluni, interview.

25  GRYT Health has updated their website. Jane's story is now located at: https://grythealth.com/resources/hub/jane-marczewskis-nightbirde-breast-cancer-story.

26  Jane Marczewski passed away while I was writing this chapter in 2022. RIP Jane. It's okay now.

27  America's Got Talent, season 16, episode 2, "Auditions 2: Jane Marczewski," aired June 8, 2021, https://www.nbc.com/americas-got-talent/video/auditions-2/4374761.

28  Craig, interview.

29  Carolyn O'Hara, "How to Tell a Great Story," *Harvard Business Review*, July 30, 2014, https://hbr.org/2014/07/how-to-tell-a-great-story.

30  Arabeth Balasko, interview with the author, November 7, 2019.

31  Howard Behar with Janet Goldstein, *It's Not About the Coffee: Leadership Principles from a Life at Starbucks* (New York: Portfolio, 2007) p. 65; Kevin Eikenberry, Leadership and Learning: Leadership and a Cup of Coffee with Howard Behar, https://blog. kevineikenberry.com/podcast/leadership-cup-coffee-howard-behar/.

32  Deepak Chopra, *The Seven Spiritual Laws of Success: A Practical Guide to the Fulfillment of Your Dreams* (Amber-Allen Publishing, 1994), p. 29–30.

33  Julian B. Rotter, "Interpersonal Trust, Trustworthiness, and Gullibility," *American Psychologist* 35., no. 1 (1980): 1–7, https://doi. org/10.1037/0003-066X.35.1.1, p. 26.

34    Paul J. Zak, "The Neuroscience of Trust," *Harvard Business Review*,
      January 2017, https://hbr.org/2017/01/the-neuroscience-of-trust.

35    Bob Easton, interview with the author, August 10, 2019.

36    Chris Lamb, interview with the author, August 22, 2019.

## Chapter 11

1     Manny Ocasio, interview with the author, January 7, 2020.

2     Avatar Wiki, s.v. "I See You," accessed June 7, 2022, https://james-
      camerons-avatar.fandom.com/wiki/I_See_You#Na.27vi_Greeting.

3     Roy F. Baumeister and Mark R. Leary, "The Need to Belong:
      Desire for Interpersonal Attachments as a Fundamental Human
      Motivation," *Psychological Bulletin* 117, no. 3 (1995): 497–529, https://
      doi.org/10.1037/0033-2909.117.3.497.

4     Andrew Steptoe et al., "Loneliness and Neuroendocrine,
      Cardiovascular, and Inflammatory Stress Responses in Middle-Aged
      Men and Women," *Psychoneuroendocrinology* 29, no. 5 (June 2004):
      593–611, https://doi.org/10.1016/S0306-4530(03)00086-6.

5     Rene A. Spitz, "Hospitalism: An Inquiry into the Genesis of
      Psychiatric Conditions in Early Childhood," *The Psychoanalytic Study
      of the Child* 1, no. 1 (1945): 53–74, https://doi.org/10.1080/00797308
      .1945.11823126; UNICEF International Child Development Center,
      "Children at Risk in Central and Eastern Europe: Perils and Promises,"
      Economies in Transition Studies Regional Monitoring Report No. 4
      (1997), https://www.unicef-irc.org/publications/pdf/monee4.pdf.

6     Julianne Holt-Lundstad, Timothy B. Smith, and J. Bradley Layton,
      "Social Relationships and Mortality Risk: A Meta-Analytic Review,"
      *PLoS Med* 7, no. 7 (July 2010): e1000316, https://doi.org/10.1371/
      journal.pmed.1000316.

7     Robert Waldinger, "What Makes a Good Life? Lessons from the
      Longest Study on Happiness," TED Talk, January 25, 2016, 12:46,
      https://www.youtube.com/watch?v=8KkKuTCFvzI.

8     *Better Call Saul*, season 2, episode 4, "Gloves Off," created by Vince
      Gilligan and Peter Gould, produced by Bob Odenkirk, Nina Jack,
      and Diane Mercer, air date March 7, 2016, Sony Pictures Home
      Entertainment.

9   Elizabeth Alexander, *Crave Radiance: New and Selected Poems 1990–2010* (Graywolf Press, 2012) p. 185.

10  Reward Gateway, "The Top Three Demotivators of the Workplace: Lack of Recognition, Feeling Invisible or Undervalued, and Bad Managers," press release, October 23, 2018, https://www.prnewswire.com/news-releases/the-top-three-demotivators-of-the-workplace-lack-of-recognition-feeling-invisible-or-undervalued-and-bad-managers-300735823.html.

11  Armando Rodriguez-Pérez et al., "Infra-Humanization of Outgroups Throughout the World. The Role of Similarity, Intergroup Friendship, Knowledge of the Outgroup, and Status," *Anales de Psicología* 27, no. 3 (2011): 679–687, https://revistas.um.es/analesps/article/download/135271/123471/517061.

12  Dora Capozza, Gian Antonio Di Bernardo, and Rossella Falvo, "Intergroup Contact and Outgroup Humanization: Is the Causal Relationship Uni- or Bidirectional?" *PLoS One* 12, no. 1 (2017), https://doi.org/10.1371/journal.pone.0170554.

13  Nick Haslam, "Subhuman, Inhuman, and Superhuman: Contrasting Humans with Nonhumans in Three Cultures," *Social Cognition* 26, no. 2 (April 2008), https://doi.org/10.1521/soco.2008.26.2.248.

14  Brock Bastian and Nick Haslam, "Experiencing Dehumanization: Cognitive and Emotional Effects of Everyday Dehumanization," *Basic and Applied Social Psychology* 33, no. 4 (2011): 295–303, https://doi.org/10.1080/01973533.2011.614132; Jacques-Philippe Leyens et al., "Psychological Essentialism and the Differential Attribution of Uniquely Human Emotions to Ingroups and Outgroups," *European Journal of Social Psychology* 31, no. 4 (July 2001): 395–411, https://doi.org/10.1002/ejsp.50.

15  David Livingstone Smith, *Less Than Human: Why We Demean, Enslave, and Exterminate Others* (St. Martin's Griffin, 2012).

16  Information about Dr. Philip Zimbardo's prison experiment at Stanford University available at: https://www.prisonexp.org.

17  David M. Markowitz et al., "Dehumanization During the COVID-19 Pandemic," *Frontiers in Psychology* 12 (February 2021), https://doi.org/10.3389/fpsyg.2021.634543.

18    Luke Barr, "Hate Crimes Against Asians Rose 76% in 2020 Amid Pandemic, FBI Says," ABC News, October 25, 2021, https://abcnews. go.com/US/hate-crimes-asians-rose-76-2020-amid-pandemic/ story?id=80746198.

19    Darrell West, "How Employers Use Technology to Surveil Employees," *TechTank*, Brookings Institute, January 5, 2021, https:// www.brookings.edu/blog/techtank/2021/01/05/how-employers-use-technology-to-surveil-employees.

20    Bastian and Haslam, "Experiencing Dehumanization."

21    Matías Arriagad-Venegas, David Pérez-Jorge, and Eva Ariño-Mateo, "The Ingroup–Outgroup Relationship Influences Their Humanity: A Moderation Analysis of Status and Gender," *Frontiers in Psychology* 12 (November 2021), https://doi.org/10.3389/fpsyg.2021.725898.

22    Susan David, "I See You," LinkedIn, December 17, 2019, https://www. linkedin.com/pulse/i-see-you-susan-a-david-ph-d.

23    Balasko, interview.

24    "About Pierre," Pierre Dulaine, accessed June 7, 2022, http://www. pierredulaine.org/about-pierre.

25    *Dancing in Jaffa*, directed by Hilla Medalia (2013; New York, Pretty Pictures).

26    "About Pierre."

27    Ocasio, interview.

28    American Psychological Association Dictionary, s.v. "primacy effect," accessed June 7, 2022, https://dictionary.apa.org/primacy-effects.

29    Roderick I. Swaab, William W. Maddox, and Marwan Sinaceur, "Early Words That Work: When and How Virtual Linguistic Mimicry Facilitates Negotiation Outcomes," *Journal of Experimental Social Psychology* 47, no. 3 (May 2011): 616–621, https://doi.org/10.1016/j. jesp.2011.01.005.

30    Katherine Metcalf et al., "Mirroring to Build Trust in Digital Assistants," Apple Inc., April 2, 2019, https://arxiv.org/pdf/1904. 01664.pdf.

31    Chris Voss, "5 Tactics to Win a Negotiation, According to an FBI Agent," *Time*, May 25, 2016, https://time.com/4326364/negotiation-tactics.

32   Kerry Breen, "Peloton's Alex Toussaint Shares Inspiring Story with Carson Daly," *Today*, January 15, 2021, https://www.today.com/health/peloton-s-alex-toussaint-shares-inspiring-story-carson-daly-t205782.

33   Merriam-Webster, s.v. "peloton," accessed June 7, 2022, https://www.merriam-webster.com/dictionary/peloton.

34   John Ballard, "Why Peloton's New Subscription Plan Is a Big Red Flag," The Motley Fool, April 2, 2022, https://www.fool.com/investing/2022/04/02/why-pelotons-new-subscription-plan-big-red-flag.

35   Peloton, Shareholder Letter, Q4 2021, accessed June 7, 2022, https://investor.onepeloton.com/static-files/4836b73e-6e63-4517-a3cd-86c45ea98e68.

36   Juliet Bourke, *Which Two Heads Are Better Than One?: The Extraordinary Power of Diversity of Thinking and Inclusive Leadership*, 2nd Edition (Australian Institute of Company Directors, 2021).

37   Juliet Bourke, "The Diversity and Inclusion Revolution: Eight Powerful Truths," *Deloitte Review* 22 (January 2018), https://www2.deloitte.com/us/en/insights/deloitte-review/issue-22/diversity-and-inclusion-at-work-eight-powerful-truths.html.

38   Peter Bailinson et al., "Understanding Organizational Barriers to a More Inclusive Workplace," McKinsey & Company, June 23, 2020, https://www.mckinsey.com/business-functions/people-and-organizational-performance/our-insights/understanding-organizational-barriers-to-a-more-inclusive-workplace.

39   Gena Cox, *Leading Inclusion: Drive Change Your Employees Can See and Feel* (Page Two, 2022), p. 75, 77.

40   Stand Out in 90 Seconds was created by Ashwin Krishnan and can be accessed at: https://standoutin90sec.com.

41   Richard E. Boyatzis, "Competencies in the 21st Century," *Journal of Management Development* 27, no. 1 (2008), https://doi.org/10.1108/02621710810840730.

42   William A. Gentry, Todd J. Weber, and Golzan Sadri, "Empathy in the Workplace: A Tool for Effective Leadership," white paper, Center for Creative Leadership, revised November 2011,

https://cclinnovation.org/wp-content/uploads/2020/03/
empathyintheworkplace.pdf.

43    Graham Binks, interview with the author, June 27, 2019.

44    Marshall Goldsmith, interview with the author, September 24, 2019.

45    Easton, interview.

46    Sadie F. Dingfelder, "How Artists See," *Monitor on Psychology* 41, no. 2
      (February 2010): 40, https://www.apa.org/monitor/2010/02/artists.

47    Tolentino, interview.

### Chapter 12

1    Zikakis, interview.

2    For SMART goal examples, see Indeed Editorial Team, "How Do
     You Set SMART Goals? Definition and Examples," Indeed, May 23,
     2022, https://www.indeed.com/career-advice/career-development/
     smart-goals; Eileen Azzara, "SMART Goal Examples for Developing
     Leadership Competencies," LinkedIn, December 30, 2016, https://
     www.linkedin.com/pulse/smart-goal-examples-developing-
     leadership-eileen-azzara.

### Conclusion

1    Croom, interview.

# index